Guide to Food Storage

Follow this guide for food storage, and you can be sure that what's in your freezer, refrigerator, and pantry is fresh-tasting and ready to use in recipes.

In the Freezer (at -10° to 0° F)

DAIRY

Cheese, hard	6 months
Cheese, soft	6 months
Egg substitute, unopened	1 year
Egg whites	1 year
Egg yolks	1 year
Ice cream, sherbet	1 month

FRUITS AND VEGETABLES

Commercially frozen fruits	1 year
Commercially frozen vegetables	8 to 12 months

MEATS, POULTRY, AND SEAFOOD

Beef, Lamb, Pork, and Veal

Chops, uncooked	4 to 6 months
Ground and stew meat, uncooked	3 to 4 months
Ham, fully cooked, half	1 to 2 months
Roasts, uncooked	4 to 12 months
Steaks, uncooked	6 to 12 months

Poultry

All cuts, cooked	4 months
Boneless or bone-in pieces, uncooked	9 months

Seafood

Fish, fatty, uncooked	2 to 3 months
Fish, lean, uncooked	6 months

In the Refrigerator (at 34° to 40° F)

DAIRY

Butter	1 to 3 months
Buttermilk	1 to 2 weeks
Cheese, hard, wedge, opened	6 months
Cheese, semihard, block, opened	3 to 4 weeks
Cream cheese, fat-free, light, and ⅓-less-fat	2 weeks
Egg substitute, opened	3 days
Fresh eggs in shell	3 to 5 weeks

MEATS, POULTRY, AND SEAFOOD

Beef, Lamb, Pork, and Veal

Ground and stew meat, uncooked	1 to 2 days
Roasts, uncooked	3 to 5 days
Steaks and chops, uncooked	3 to 5 days

Chicken, Turkey, and Seafood

All cuts, uncooked	1 to 2 days

FRUITS AND VEGETABLES

Apples, beets, cabbage, carrots, celery, citrus fruits, eggplant, and parsnips	2 to 3 weeks
Apricots, asparagus, berries, cauliflower, cucumbers, mushrooms, okra, peaches, pears, peas, peppers, plums, salad greens, and summer squash	2 to 4 days
Corn, husked	1 day

In the Pantry (keep these at room temperature for 6 to 12 months)

BAKING AND COOKING STAPLES

Baking powder
Biscuit and baking mixes
Broth, canned
Cooking spray
Honey
Mayonnaise, fat-free, low-fat, and light (unopened)
Milk, canned evaporated fat-free
Milk, nonfat dry powder

Mustard, prepared (unopened)
Oils, olive and vegetable
Pasta, dried
Peanut butter
Rice, instant and regular
Salad dressings, bottled (unopened)
Seasoning sauces, bottled
Tuna, canned

FRUITS, LEGUMES, AND VEGETABLES

Fruits, canned
Legumes (beans, lentils, peas), dried or canned
Tomato products, canned
Vegetables, canned

WeightWatchers®

5ingredient
15minute
cookbook

Oxmoor
House®

ISBN-13: 978-0-8487-3227-1
ISBN-10: 0-8487-3227-8
Library of Congress Control Number: 2007942030

Printed in the United States of America
First Edition 2002. Second Edition 2008

Be sure to check with your health-care provider before making any changes in your diet.

Weight Watchers, **POINTS**, and the Core Plan are registered trademarks of Weight Watchers International, Inc., and are used under license by Oxmoor House, Inc.

Oxmoor House, Inc.
Editor in Chief: Nancy Fitzpatrick Wyatt
Executive Editor: Katherine M. Eakin
Art Director: Keith McPherson
Managing Editor: Allison Long Lowery

Weight Watchers® 5 Ingredient 15 Minute Cookbook
Development Editor: Andrea C. Kirkland, M.S., R.D.
Project Editor: Diane Rose
Senior Designer: Emily Albright Parrish
Copy Chief: L. Amanda Owens
Editorial Assistants: Kevin Pearsall, Vanessa Rusch Thomas
Director, Test Kitchens: Elizabeth Tyler Austin
Assistant Director, Test Kitchens: Julie Christopher
Test Kitchens Professionals: Jane Chambliss; Patricia Michaud; Kathleen Royal Phillips; Catherine Crowell Steele; Ashley T. Strickland; Kate Wheeler, R.D.
Photography Director: Jim Bathie
Senior Photo Stylist: Kay E. Clarke
Associate Photo Stylist: Katherine G. Eckert
Director of Production: Laura Lockhart
Production Manager: Theresa Beste-Farley

Contributors
Compositor: Carol O. Loria
Copy Editor: Dolores Hydock
Indexer: Mary Ann Laurens
Recipe Development: Gretchen Feldtman Brown, R.D.; Maureen Callahan, R.D.; Jennifer Cofield; Caroline Grant, M.S., R.D.; Jackie Mills, R.D.
Interns: Tracey Apperson, Cory L. Bordonaro, Carol Corbin, Erin Loudy
Food Stylists: Ana Price Kelly, Debby Maugans
Photographers: Beau Gustafson, Lee Harrelson
Photo Stylists: Melanie J. Clarke

Cover: Bacon and Sun-Dried Tomato Alfredo Pasta, page 112

To order additional publications, call 1-800-765-6400.
For more books to enrich your life,
visit **oxmoorhouse.com**
To search, savor, and share thousands of recipes,
visit **myrecipes.com**

Contents

Great Meals in Minutes

You're only minutes away from enjoying wholesome home-cooked meals any night of the week with this all-new *5 Ingredient 15 Minute Cookbook* from Weight Watchers® Books. You'll turn to these quick and delicious recipes over and over again.

Time-saving Tips and Techniques

The Weight Watchers Books Test Kitchen staff share some of their favorite tried-and-true tips and techniques for preparing great-tasting, nutritious food fast!

Select the best recipes.

A lot of these top-rated recipes only require 5 ingredients or less (excluding water, cooking spray, salt, pepper, and optional ingredients). Others have a few more ingredients but go from grocery bag to dinner table in 15 minutes or less. And many fall into both categories.

Use menus to save time when planning meals.

Each menu in this book includes a main-dish recipe plus either a side-dish recipe or a "serve with" suggestion, such as a fruit, vegetable, bread, or grain to round out the meal. The *POINTS*® values per serving are included with every menu and every recipe.

Use a smart shopping list.

Ingredients for menus are listed following the basic layout of a large supermarket: produce, bakery, deli, nuts and dried fruit, canned foods and condiments, grains, baking ingredients, alcohol, dairy, frozen foods, and refrigerated meats.

Purchase nutritious convenience products.

• **Prepared produce:** Packages of prechopped, preshredded, presliced, pretrimmed, and prewashed fruits and vegetables shave minutes off the prep time. Always check the freshness date, and look closely for signs of deterioration.

• **Refrigerated potatoes:** Packages of refrigerated potatoes are ready to cook when purchased—just follow the cooking directions on the package. Look for them in a variety of forms—diced, mashed, quartered, shredded, and sliced.

• **Precooked rice:** Stock up on shelf-stable precooked whole-grain brown rice and long-grain white rice for supersimple side dishes. Heat in the microwave and serve alone, or toss in your favorite spices, herbs, or chopped vegetables.

• **Rotisserie chicken:** Roasted whole chickens are available in most supermarkets and are a good choice for low-fat recipes. The fat savings are substantial when you remove and discard the skin before chopping or shredding the chicken to use in a recipe. One 2-pound rotisserie chicken yields about 3 cups of chopped or shredded chicken. Rotisserie chicken can be high in sodium. If sodium is a concern, substitute plain roasted chicken in the recipes that call for a rotisserie chicken.

Keep flavor-rich ingredients on hand.

• **Highly flavored cheese:** Parmesan cheese is an excellent cheese for light cooking. Preshredded fresh Parmesan is fine for convenience, but for the best flavor, grate or shave the cheese yourself. A cheese plane or a swivel-blade peeler works well for creating large shavings of cheese. Store a wedge lightly wrapped in plastic wrap in the refrigerator for up to 6 months.

- **Freshly ground black pepper:** Freshly ground black peppercorns offer a sharper, more pungent bite than the typical finely ground black pepper packaged in a tin or can. For the best flavor, grind whole black peppercorns just before you need them. Ten full cranks of a pepper mill will produce about ¼ teaspoon of ground black pepper.
- **Fresh citrus:** Freshly squeezed lemon, lime, and orange juice and grated rind can balance and brighten the flavor in all types of foods, from savory to sweet.
- **Fresh herbs:** Fresh herbs, such as basil, cilantro, mint, thyme, and parsley, are easy to find, and they infuse recipes with flavor and aroma. Look for these herbs year-round in the produce section of your supermarket. To keep fresh herbs for up to a week, trim about ¼ inch from the stems, and rinse the herbs with cold water. Loosely wrap herbs in a damp paper towel; then seal them in a zip-top plastic bag filled with air. Or place herb stems in a glass with water (let water cover about 1 inch of the stem ends; change the water every other day).

Experiment with quick, low-fat cooking techniques.

- **Pan-sear:** Pan-sear meat, seafood, and poultry to create a golden brown crust and retain juices. The key to the perfect pan-sear is a hot skillet. You should hear a loud sizzle or pop as soon as you place the food in the skillet. Resist the temptation to move the food once it is in the skillet. A golden brown crust requires at least 3 uninterrupted minutes of heat before turning.
- **Deglaze:** After searing, deglaze the pan with water, broth, fruit juice, vinegar, or wine to create a richly flavored sauce. Scrape the bottom of the pan to loosen the brown crunchy bits left behind.
- **Grill:** Grilling adds smokiness and intensifies the natural flavors in a variety of foods. It is a simple method that makes meat, fish, and poultry succulent and vegetables crisp-tender. To get the best results, preheat the grill before cooking and be sure to use tongs or a spatula to turn food. Don't pierce the food with a fork or knife because this allows flavorful juices to escape.

Equip the kitchen with time-saving tools and appliances.

- **Garlic press:** Use a garlic press when a recipe calls for crushed or minced garlic. This tool provides the easiest and most efficient method for crushing garlic and can be used instead of mincing garlic with a knife.
- **Kitchen shears:** Use a pair of kitchen shears for small mincing or chopping jobs instead of pulling out a knife and cutting board. Kitchen shears are ideal for a variety of tasks—from snipping herbs and chopping canned vegetables in the can to chopping dried fruit and trimming fat from chicken breasts.
- **Flat-sided meat mallet:** Cut the cook time and produce tender and moist chicken-breast dishes by using a flat-sided meat mallet. Just place skinless, boneless chicken breasts between two layers of heavy-duty plastic wrap and pound to an even thickness—about ¼ to ½ inch thick.
- **Microwave:** Use your microwave to heat precooked products such as bacon, rice, and mashed potatoes; defrost frozen vegetables; and steam fresh vegetables while you are working on a different step of a recipe.
- **Slow cooker:** Set aside a few minutes in the morning to prepare the ingredients. Toss them into the slow cooker, turn it on, and go about your day. Then come home to a complete mouthwatering meal waiting for you.

About the Recipes

Weight Watchers® 5 Ingredient 15 Minute Cookbook gives you the nutrition facts you need to stay on track. Every recipe in this book includes a *POINTS®* value. We use a ☑. to identify recipes that fall within the Core Plan®. For more information on Weight Watchers, see page 5.

Each recipe has a complete list of nutrients,

including calories, fat, saturated fat, protein, carbohydrates, dietary fiber, cholesterol, iron, sodium, and calcium, as well as a serving size and the number of servings. This information makes it easy for you to use the recipes in any weight-loss program that you may choose to follow. Measurements are abbreviated g (grams) and mg (milligrams). Nutritional values used in our calculations either come from The Food Processor, Version 7.5 (ESHA Research), or are provided by food manufacturers.

Numbers are based on these assumptions:
• Unless otherwise indicated, meat, poultry, and fish always refer to skinned, boned, and cooked servings.
• When we give a range for an ingredient (3 to 3½ cups flour, for instance), we calculate using the lesser amount.
• Some alcohol calories evaporate during heating; the analysis reflects this.
• Only the amount of marinade absorbed by the food is used in calculations.
• Garnishes and optional ingredients are not included in an analysis.

Safety note: Cooking spray should never be used near direct heat. Always remove a pan from heat before spraying it with cooking spray.

A note on Diabetic Exchanges: You may notice that the nutrient analysis for each recipe does not include Diabetic Exchanges. Most dietitians and diabetes educators are now teaching people with diabetes to count total carbohydrates at each meal and snack, rather than counting exchanges.

Counting carbohydrates gives people with diabetes more flexibility in their food choices and seems to be an effective way to manage blood glucose.

Almost all of our recipes can be incorporated into a diabetic diet by using the carbohydrate amount in the nutrient analysis and incorporating that into the carbohydrate amount recommended by your physician.

Choose Your Food Plan

Weight Watchers offers two approaches to making wise food choices and allows you to switch back and forth between plans for maximum flexibility and lasting weight loss.

The Flex Plan is based on the Weight Watchers *POINTS* Weight-Loss System.
• Every food has a *POINTS* value that is based on calories, fat grams, fiber grams, and portion size.
• Members who use the Flex Plan keep track of *POINTS* values and maintain their daily *POINTS* values within a set range called the *POINTS* Target.
• You can enjoy a full range of food options at home, on the go, or when dining out.

The Core Plan offers foods from a list of wholesome, nutritious foods from all groups—fruits and vegetables; grains and starches; lean meats, fish, and poultry; eggs; and dairy products.
• No measuring or counting is required, as Core Foods provide eating satisfaction and fullness without empty calories.
• For the occasional treat, you can also eat foods outside of this list in a controlled amount.

Appetizers & Beverages

Grocery List

1 whole garlic head

1 small bunch fresh rosemary

1 (8-ounce) carton fat-free sour cream

Check staples: fat-free milk, light mayonnaise, Dijon mustard, and salt

Creamy Rosemary Dip

prep: 5 minutes

POINTS value: 1

Fresh rosemary plus a few pantry items create a winning dip that's perfect for your next dinner party or afternoon snack. Dress up this versatile recipe by serving it alongside fresh asparagus spears or whole green beans steamed until they are crisp-tender.

⅓ cup fat-free sour cream

2½ tablespoons light mayonnaise

2 tablespoons fat-free milk

2 teaspoons Dijon mustard

1 garlic clove, minced

1 teaspoon chopped fresh rosemary

⅛ teaspoon salt

1. Combine all ingredients in a small bowl; stir well. Serve immediately, or cover and chill until ready to serve. Yield: 5 servings (serving size: about 2 tablespoons).

Per serving: CALORIES 46 (52% from fat); FAT 2.7g (saturated fat 0.6g); PROTEIN 1.1g; CARBOHYDRATES 4.1g; FIBER 0g; CHOLESTEROL 4mg; IRON 0.1mg; SODIUM 182mg; CALCIUM 33mg

White Bean Dip

prep: 6 minutes

POINTS value: 1

Serve this velvety dip with pita wedges or crunchy vegetables, such as baby carrots, cucumber slices, or red bell pepper strips, or as a spread on turkey, chicken, or lamb pita sandwiches.

- 1 (15.5-ounce) can cannellini beans, rinsed and drained
- 7 mint leaves
- 1 tablespoon lemon juice
- 1 tablespoon olive oil
- 1 garlic clove
- ¼ teaspoon salt
- ⅛ teaspoon black pepper

1. Process all ingredients in a blender until smooth, stopping to scrape down sides as needed. Serve immediately, or cover and chill until ready to serve. Yield: 10 servings (serving size: 2 tablespoons).

Per serving: CALORIES 33 (41% from fat); FAT 1.5g (saturated fat 0.2g); PROTEIN 1g; CARBOHYDRATES 3.8g; FIBER 1g; CHOLESTEROL 0mg; IRON 0.4mg; SODIUM 90mg; CALCIUM 9mg

Grocery List

1 small bunch fresh mint

1 small lemon

1 whole garlic head

1 (15.5-ounce) can cannellini beans

Check staples: olive oil, salt, and black pepper

Grilled Corn and Black Bean Salsa ☑.

prep: 2 minutes • **cook:** 12 minutes   *POINTS* value: 0

Place the corn directly on the grill rack to cook. The kernels will develop a slightly charred golden color on the outside and a smoky grilled flavor on the inside. Toss with black beans and tomato for a quick salsa to serve with baked tortilla chips. Increase the serving size to 1 cup and the salsa becomes a side dish with a *POINTS* value of 1 to serve alongside grilled fish, meat, or chicken.

  2 medium ears shucked corn
Cooking spray
½ teaspoon salt
¼ teaspoon pepper
  1 (15-ounce) can black beans, rinsed and drained
  1 large tomato, chopped
  2 tablespoons red wine vinegar
  1 teaspoon olive oil
½ teaspoon ground cumin

1. Prepare grill.

2. Coat 2 ears corn with cooking spray; sprinkle with salt and pepper. Place corn on grill rack; cover and grill 6 minutes on each side or until slightly charred.

3. While corn cooks, combine beans and next 4 ingredients in a medium bowl. Cut corn off cob, and add to bowl; toss well. Yield: 20 servings (serving size: ¼ cup).

Per serving: CALORIES 19 (19% from fat); FAT 0.4g (saturated fat 0.1g); PROTEIN 0.9g; CARBOHYDRATES 3.7g; FIBER 1g; CHOLESTEROL 0mg; IRON 0.3mg; SODIUM 83mg; CALCIUM 6mg

Strawberry-Orange Pepper Jelly Spread

prep: 4 minutes • **cook:** 25 seconds   *POINTS* value: 3

Serve this spicy jelly and cream cheese with slices of apple or pear rather than the traditional buttery crackers. You can also serve the spread with turkey, chicken, or pork.

¼   cup strawberry fruit spread (such as Polaner All Fruit)
½   teaspoon grated orange rind
¼   teaspoon crushed red pepper
½   cup (4 ounces) ⅓-less-fat cream cheese

1. Combine fruit spread, orange rind, and crushed red pepper in a small microwave-safe bowl. Microwave at HIGH 25 to 30 seconds; remove from microwave.

2. Serve pepper jelly spread with cream cheese. Yield: 4 servings (serving size: 1 tablespoon pepper jelly spread and 2 tablespoons cream cheese).

Per serving: CALORIES 113 (49% from fat); FAT 6.1g (saturated fat 4.1g); PROTEIN 3.2g; CARBOHYDRATES 11.4g; FIBER 0.1g; CHOLESTEROL 20mg; IRON 0mg; SODIUM 130mg; CALCIUM 21mg

Grocery List

1 small orange

1 (10-ounce) jar strawberry fruit spread (such as Polaner All Fruit)

1 (8-ounce) block ⅓-less-fat cream cheese

Check staples: crushed red pepper

pictured on page 34

Mediterranean Goat Cheese Spread

prep: 4 minutes • **cook:** 1 minute, 15 seconds • **other:** 10 minutes   *POINTS* value: 2

Gently fold the olives and tomatoes into the cheese mixture; overmixing may turn the cheese spread an unappetizing purplish pink color. Serve this spread on melba toast rounds or toasted wheat baguette slices.

Grocery List

1 (3-ounce) package sun-dried tomatoes, packed without oil

1 (7-ounce) jar pitted kalamata olives

1 (3-ounce) package goat cheese

1 (8-ounce) carton fat-free sour cream

Check staples: salt

     4   sun-dried tomatoes, packed without oil
    ¼   cup water
    ¼   cup (2 ounces) goat cheese
     3   tablespoons fat-free sour cream
    ⅛   teaspoon salt
     6   pitted kalamata olives, finely chopped

1. Combine tomatoes and water in a microwave-safe bowl. Microwave at HIGH 1 minute or until water boils. Remove from microwave; cover with plastic wrap and let stand 10 minutes to soften.

2. While sun-dried tomatoes stand, place goat cheese in a microwave-safe bowl; micro-wave at HIGH 15 seconds or until soft. Add sour cream and salt, stirring until well blended; fold in olives.

3. Drain tomatoes; finely chop, and fold into goat cheese mixture. Serve immediately, or cover and chill until ready to serve. Yield: 4 servings (serving size: 2 tablespoons).

Per serving: CALORIES 101 (60% from fat); FAT 6.7g (saturated fat 3.8g); PROTEIN 5.5g; CARBOHYDRATES 4.7g; FIBER 0.6g; CHOLESTEROL 16mg; IRON 0.6mg; SODIUM 226mg; CALCIUM 146mg

Jalapeño, Rice, and Cheese Bites

prep: 6 minutes • **cook:** 15 minutes • **other:** 3 minutes   *POINTS* value: 1

You can make this appetizer ahead. Bake and refrigerate; then reheat in a 300° oven for about 10 minutes just before serving.

1   cup precooked whole-grain brown rice
½   cup (2 ounces) reduced-fat shredded sharp Cheddar cheese, divided
½   teaspoon salt
2   large egg whites, lightly beaten
2   medium jalapeño peppers, seeded and minced
Cooking spray
1   (2-ounce) jar diced pimiento, drained

1. Preheat oven to 350°.

2. Combine rice and 2 tablespoons cheese in a medium bowl; add next 3 ingredients, stirring until blended.

3. Spoon mixture evenly into 12 miniature muffin cups coated with cooking spray. Bake at 350° for 15 minutes. Remove from oven; sprinkle with remaining cheese, and top with pimiento. Let stand 3 minutes; gently remove from pan. Serve warm. Yield: 12 servings (serving size: 1 bite).

Per serving: CALORIES 38 (33% from fat); FAT 1.4g (saturated fat 0.7g); PROTEIN 2.3g; CARBOHYDRATES 4g; FIBER 0.3g; CHOLESTEROL 3mg; IRON 0.1mg; SODIUM 148mg; CALCIUM 35mg

Grocery List

2 medium jalapeño peppers

1 (2-ounce) jar diced pimiento

1 (8.8-ounce) package precooked whole-grain brown rice

1 (8-ounce) package reduced-fat shredded sharp Cheddar cheese

Check staples: eggs, cooking spray, and salt

Mini Ham and Spinach Quiches

prep: 10 minutes • **cook:** 16 minutes   *POINTS* value: 1

Prepare these mini quiches for your next brunch gathering. Serve with an assortment of fresh fruit, such as seedless grapes, cubed melon, and pineapple.

9 (1.5-ounce) slices hearty white bread
Butter-flavored cooking spray
½ cup egg substitute
¼ cup frozen chopped spinach, thawed, drained, and squeezed dry
¼ cup diced ham
¼ cup (1 ounce) reduced-fat shredded sharp Cheddar cheese
¼ teaspoon pepper
⅛ teaspoon salt

1. Preheat oven to 400°.
2. Cut 2 (2-inch) circles out of each bread slice; press circles into 18 miniature muffin cups coated with cooking spray. Coat bread with cooking spray. Bake at 400° for 5 minutes.
3. While bread cooks, combine egg substitute and next 5 ingredients in a small bowl. Spoon egg mixture evenly onto bread in each cup. Bake at 400° for 11 minutes or until egg mixture is set. Yield: 18 servings (serving size: 1 mini quiche).

Per serving: CALORIES 68 (15% from fat); FAT 1.1g (saturated fat 0.2g); PROTEIN 3.2g; CARBOHYDRATES 11.3g; FIBER 0.6g; CHOLESTEROL 3mg; IRON 0.9mg; SODIUM 209mg; CALCIUM 38mg

Pizza Pockets

prep: 13 minutes • **cook:** 12 minutes   *POINTS* value: 3

A can of reduced-fat crescent roll dough jump-starts these kid-friendly pepperoni pizza snacks. Allow your kids to help sprinkle the ingredients for the stuffing on top of the dough before you fold it into triangles. Serve the pockets with your favorite marinara sauce.

   1 (8-ounce) can refrigerated reduced-fat crescent dinner roll dough
   ¼ cup chopped turkey pepperoni
   ¼ cup chopped green bell pepper
   2 tablespoons shredded part-skim mozzarella cheese
   Cooking spray
   ½ cup marinara sauce

1. Preheat oven to 375°.

2. Unroll half of dough and separate into 2 rectangles, gently pressing seams together with fingertips. Cut rectangle into 4 even squares. Repeat procedure with remaining half of dough.

3. Divide pepperoni, bell pepper, and cheese evenly on center of each square. Fold 1 corner over to opposite corner, creating a triangle; press edges together firmly to seal.

4. Place pockets on a baking sheet coated with cooking spray; coat tops with cooking spray. Bake at 375° for 12 minutes or until golden brown. Serve with marinara sauce. Yield: 8 servings (serving size: 1 pocket and 1 tablespoon marinara sauce).

Per serving: CALORIES 128 (41% from fat); FAT 5.7g (saturated fat 1.4g); PROTEIN 4.2g; CARBOHYDRATES 14.1g; FIBER 0.1g; CHOLESTEROL 7mg; IRON 0.1mg; SODIUM 393mg; CALCIUM 15mg

Grocery List

1 small green bell pepper

1 (24-ounce) jar marinara sauce

1 (8-ounce) can refrigerated reduced-fat crescent dinner roll dough

1 (4-ounce) package shredded part-skim mozzarella cheese

1 (6-ounce) package turkey pepperoni

Check staples: cooking spray

Sun-Dried Tomato and Olive Crescent Rolls

prep: 18 minutes • **cook:** 12 minutes   *POINTS* value: 2

Served warm, these boldly seasoned crescent rolls received rave reviews from our Test Kitchen staff. These rolls are versatile and can be served as an appetizer or as an accompaniment to soup or salad.

¼ cup grated fresh Parmesan cheese
¼ cup chopped drained oil-packed sun-dried tomato halves (about 5)
¼ cup chopped pitted kalamata olives
2 teaspoons minced fresh oregano
1 (8-ounce) can refrigerated reduced-fat crescent dinner roll dough
Cooking spray

1. Preheat oven to 375°.

2. Combine first 4 ingredients in a medium bowl.

3. Unroll dough onto a smooth surface; sprinkle Parmesan cheese mixture evenly over dough, pressing gently with fingers. Cut dough along perforated edges to form triangles; cut each triangle into 2 smaller equal triangles.

4. Roll up triangles, starting at wide end. Place on a baking sheet coated with cooking spray, pointed end down. Bake at 375° for 12 minutes or until golden brown. Serve immediately. Yield: 16 servings (serving size: 1 crescent roll).

Per serving: CALORIES 68 (48% from fat); FAT 3.6g (saturated fat 0.9g); PROTEIN 1.9g; CARBOHYDRATES 6.7g; FIBER 0.1g; CHOLESTEROL 1mg; IRON 0.1mg; SODIUM 189mg; CALCIUM 27mg

Asian Lettuce Wraps

prep: 6 minutes • **cook:** 7 minutes   *POINTS* value: 1

You can serve these wraps buffet-style. Arrange the lettuce leaves on a large platter and spoon the chicken mixture into a bowl. Let your guests assemble their own wraps. Serve with an Asian dipping sauce or peanut sauce, if desired.

Cooking spray
¾ pound ground chicken
½ cup broccoli slaw
 2 garlic cloves, minced
¼ teaspoon crushed red pepper
 2 tablespoons diced water chestnuts
 3 tablespoons light sesame ginger dressing
20 medium Boston lettuce leaves

1. Heat a nonstick skillet over medium-high heat. Coat pan with cooking spray. Add chicken, slaw, and garlic; cook 6 minutes or until chicken is browned, stirring to crumble. Reduce heat to low, and stir in red pepper, water chestnuts, and dressing. Cook until thoroughly heated.

2. Fill each lettuce leaf with 2 tablespoons chicken mixture. Serve immediately.
Yield: 20 servings (serving size: 1 wrap).

Per serving: CALORIES 33 (55% from fat); FAT 2g (saturated fat 0.6g); PROTEIN 3.1g; CARBOHYDRATES 1g; FIBER 0.2g; CHOLESTEROL 21mg; IRON 0.3mg; SODIUM 42mg; CALCIUM 10mg

Grocery List

1 whole garlic head

1 (12-ounce) package broccoli slaw

2 heads Boston lettuce

1 (8-ounce) can diced water chestnuts

1 (16-ounce) bottle light sesame ginger dressing

¾ pound ground chicken

Check staples: cooking spray and crushed red pepper

Chicken Tenders with Pita Coating

prep: 8 minutes • **cook:** 15 minutes   *POINTS* value: 2

You can use whatever flavor of pita chips you prefer. In addition to the Parmesan, garlic, and herb–flavored chips, we also liked the pesto and sun-dried tomato–flavored chips.

 ½ cup egg substitute
 ½ teaspoon freshly ground black pepper
1½ cups Parmesan, garlic, and herb–flavored pita chips (such as Stacy's), finely crushed
  1 tablespoon salt-free Italian seasoning (such as Mrs. Dash)
  8 (2-ounce) chicken breast tenders
 Cooking spray
 ½ cup tomato-basil pasta sauce (such as Classico), warmed

1. Preheat oven to 400°.

2. Heat a large baking sheet in oven 5 minutes.

3. Combine egg substitute and pepper in a shallow dish. Combine chips and Italian seasoning in another shallow dish. Dip chicken in egg mixture; dredge in chip mixture. Coat preheated baking sheet with cooking spray, and place chicken on pan.

4. Bake at 400° for 15 minutes or until done. Serve with pasta sauce. Yield: 8 servings (serving size: 1 chicken breast tender and 1 tablespoon pasta sauce).

Per serving: CALORIES 79 (11% from fat); FAT 1g (saturated fat 0.1g); PROTEIN 14.3g; CARBOHYDRATES 3.7g; FIBER 0.5g; CHOLESTEROL 33mg; IRON 0.8mg; SODIUM 120mg; CALCIUM 13mg

Greek Tuna Bites

prep: 12 minutes

POINTS value: 1

A packet of lemon-pepper tuna is the key ingredient in these Mediterranean-inspired hors d'oeuvres. If you plan to prepare this recipe ahead, chill the tuna mixture by itself, and fill the shells right before serving.

1 (5-ounce) package lemon-pepper tuna
⅓ cup light mayonnaise
¼ cup chopped sun-dried tomato, packed without oil (about 5)
2 tablespoons chopped fresh dill
2 tablespoons crumbled reduced-fat feta cheese
½ teaspoon Greek seasoning
1 (2.1-ounce) package mini phyllo shells (such as Athens)
Sliced ripe olives (optional)
Dill sprigs (optional)

1. Drain tuna and pat dry with paper towels.

2. Combine tuna and next 5 ingredients in a medium bowl.

3. Fill each phyllo shell with 1 tablespoon tuna mixture. Top each with an olive slice and a dill sprig, if desired. Yield: 15 servings (serving size: 1 tuna bite).

Per serving: CALORIES 53 (51% from fat); FAT 3g (saturated fat 0.4g); PROTEIN 2.6g; CARBOHYDRATES 3.8g; FIBER 0.2g; CHOLESTEROL 6mg; IRON 0.4mg; SODIUM 115mg; CALCIUM 3mg

Grocery List

1 small bunch fresh dill

1 (3-ounce) package sun-dried tomatoes, packed without oil

1 (5-ounce) package lemon-pepper tuna

1 (2.25-ounce) can sliced ripe olives (optional)

1 (3.5-ounce) package crumbled reduced-fat feta cheese

1 (2.1-ounce) package mini phyllo shells (such as Athens)

Check staples: light mayonnaise and Greek seasoning

Grocery List

1 large lemon

1 medium red onion

1 (8-ounce) bottle light olive oil vinaigrette

1 (1.88-ounce) jar pickling spice

1 pound cooked peeled medium shrimp

Pickled Shrimp

prep: 5 minutes • **other:** 24 hours

POINTS value: 2

For a buffet appetizer, spoon the shrimp into a serving bowl and have wooden picks available for guests to spear the shrimp. As a first course, spoon the shrimp and onion mixture onto individual lettuce-lined salad plates.

1	large lemon
1½	cups water
½	cup light olive oil vinaigrette
1	teaspoon pickling spice
1	pound cooked peeled medium shrimp
1	medium red onion, thinly sliced

1. Thinly slice half of lemon; set aside. Squeeze remaining half of lemon over a small bowl to measure 2 tablespoons juice; add water, vinaigrette, and pickling spice.

2. Layer shrimp, onion, and lemon slices in a shallow dish or wide-mouthed jar. Pour lemon juice mixture over layers. Cover and refrigerate at least 24 hours. Yield: 8 servings (serving size: about 7 shrimp and ¼ cup onion).

Per serving: CALORIES 103 (35% from fat); FAT 4g (saturated fat 0.3g); PROTEIN 14.3g; CARBOHYDRATES 2.8g; FIBER 0.2g; CHOLESTEROL 115mg; IRON 1.2mg; SODIUM 283mg; CALCIUM 44mg

Turkey Flats

prep: 6 minutes

POINTS value: 3

This is a satisfying afternoon snack to help curb your appetite until dinner. You can substitute multigrain, oat, or rye crispbreads for the sesame ones, if you prefer.

  4   teaspoons light mayonnaise
  ½   teaspoon stone-ground mustard
  2   sesame crispbreads (such as Wasa)
  ¼   cup mixed baby lettuces
  2   ounces deli-sliced smoked turkey breast (such as Boar's Head)
  Dash of freshly ground black pepper

1. Spread half of mayonnaise and mustard on each crispbread. Top evenly with salad greens and turkey. Sprinkle with pepper. Yield: 2 servings (serving size: 1 turkey flat).

Per serving: CALORIES 126 (36% from fat); FAT 5.1g (saturated fat 0.7g); PROTEIN 8.7g; CARBOHYDRATES 10.2g; FIBER 0.7g; CHOLESTEROL 16mg; IRON 0.3mg; SODIUM 364mg; CALCIUM 4mg

Grocery List

1 (4-ounce) package mixed baby lettuces

2 ounces deli-sliced smoked turkey breast (such as Boar's Head)

1 (7-ounce) package sesame crispbreads (such as Wasa)

Check staples: light mayonnaise, stone-ground mustard, and black pepper

---

pictured on page 35

Cranberry Citrus Spritzer

prep: 1 minute

POINTS value: 0

Blend tart cranberry juice cocktail and diet citrus soda for a refreshing beverage. Make this drink right before serving so the soda won't lose its fizz.

1⅓   cups light cranberry juice cocktail, chilled
  4   (12-ounce) cans diet citrus soda (such as original Fresca), chilled
  4   lime wedges

1. Combine cranberry juice cocktail and soda in a pitcher. Pour evenly into 4 tall glasses filled with crushed ice, and squeeze a lime wedge over each glass. Yield: 4 servings (serving size: about 1¾ cups spritzer and 1 lime wedge).

Per serving: CALORIES 19 (0% from fat); FAT 0g (saturated fat 0g); PROTEIN 0g; CARBOHYDRATES 4.1g; FIBER 0g; CHOLESTEROL 0mg; IRON 0mg; SODIUM 27mg; CALCIUM 1mg

Grocery List

1 small lime

1 (64-ounce) bottle light cranberry juice cocktail

1 six pack (12-ounce cans) diet citrus soda (such as original Fresca)

Check staples: ice

pictured on page 123

Mango Freeze

prep: 5 minutes   *POINTS* value: 1

Serve this icy beverage to cool the heat of a hot summer day.

  2 cups mango nectar
  ½ teaspoon grated lime rind
  2 teaspoons fresh lime juice
  1 tablespoon "measures-like-sugar" calorie-free sweetener (such as Splenda)
  3 cups ice
  4 lime slices

1. Combine first 5 ingredients in a blender; process until smooth. Serve with lime slices. Yield: 4 servings (serving size: 1 cup freeze and 1 lime slice).

Per serving: CALORIES 65 (0% from fat); FAT 0.1g (saturated fat 0g); PROTEIN 0.2g; CARBOHYDRATES 16.7g; FIBER 0.4g; CHOLESTEROL 0mg; IRON 0.5mg; SODIUM 6mg; CALCIUM 22mg

Mojito Slush

prep: 10 minutes • **other:** 8 hours   *POINTS* value: 2

For a nonalcoholic version of this Cuban cocktail, replace the rum with 1 cup water and freeze, scraping occasionally, for about 3 hours.

  4 cups water
  9 ounces white rum
  1 teaspoon grated lime rind
  1 cup fresh lime juice (about 8 limes)
  ¾ cup "measures-like-sugar" calorie-free sweetener (such as Splenda)
  1 tablespoon finely chopped fresh mint
  6 lime wedges

1. Combine first 6 ingredients in a 13 x 9–inch baking dish; cover and freeze overnight. Remove mixture from freezer; scrape entire mixture with a fork until fluffy. Serve immediately with lime wedges. Or spoon into a freezer-safe container, cover, and freeze up to 1 month. Yield: 6 servings (serving size: 1 cup slush and 1 lime wedge).

Per serving: CALORIES 109 (0% from fat); FAT 0g (saturated fat 0g); PROTEIN 0.2g; CARBOHYDRATES 3.6g; FIBER 0.2g; CHOLESTEROL 0mg; IRON 0.1mg; SODIUM 1mg; CALCIUM 7mg

Desserts

Mint-Cookie Shakes

prep: 5 minutes • **cook:** 20 seconds

POINTS value: 6

We reduced the fat and calories in a fast food–style milk shake by 50 percent, but our version is just as thick and chocolaty. To soften the ice cream, microwave it at HIGH 20 seconds in its carton.

  3 cups vanilla fat-free ice cream, slightly softened
  ¼ cup fat-free milk
  ¼ teaspoon peppermint extract
 11 reduced-fat cream-filled chocolate sandwich cookies (such as Oreo), crushed

1. Place all ingredients in a blender; process just until blended, stopping as necessary to scrape down sides. Serve immediately. Yield: 4 servings (serving size: ¾ cup).

Per serving: CALORIES 279 (13% from fat); FAT 4.1g (saturated fat 0.9g); PROTEIN 6.9g; CARBOHYDRATES 53.2g; FIBER 2.4g; CHOLESTEROL 0mg; IRON 1.7mg; SODIUM 280mg; CALCIUM 166mg

Banana-Graham Ice Cream Sundaes

prep: 5 minutes
        POINTS value: 5

If you have chocolate or vanilla ice cream on hand, substitute either one for the rocky road.

1 large banana, sliced
2 cups rocky road light ice cream
3 tablespoons fat-free caramel topping
4 chocolate-covered graham crackers (such as Keebler), coarsely chopped

1. Arrange banana slices evenly in 4 small dessert dishes. Top evenly with ice cream, caramel topping, and graham crackers. Yield: 4 servings (serving size: 1 sundae).

Per serving: CALORIES 266 (24% from fat); FAT 7g (saturated fat 4g); PROTEIN 3.7g; CARBOHYDRATES 46.1g; FIBER 2.1g; CHOLESTEROL 10mg; IRON 0.6mg; SODIUM 115mg; CALCIUM 152mg

Grocery List

1 large banana

1 (12.5-ounce) package chocolate-covered graham crackers (such as Keebler)

1 (12.25-ounce) jar fat-free caramel topping

1 (1.75-quart) container rocky road light ice cream

Grocery List

4 large lemons

1 (16-ounce) package
strawberries

1 (14-ounce) can fat-free
sweetened condensed milk

1 (14.4-ounce) box low-fat
graham crackers

Check staples: "measures-like-
sugar" calorie-free sweetener
(such as Splenda)

Lemon-Berry Parfaits

prep: 10 minutes   *POINTS* value: 5

In this supersimple dessert, a refreshing, custardlike sauce is formed when fresh lemon juice combines with fat-free sweetened condensed milk. Turn the sauce into a dip for your favorite fresh fruit. One tablespoon has a *POINTS* value of 1.

1½ cups sliced strawberries
  1 tablespoon "measures-like-sugar" calorie-free sweetener (such as Splenda)
  4 large lemons
  1 (14-ounce) can fat-free sweetened condensed milk
  3 sheets low-fat graham crackers, coarsely crushed

1. Sprinkle strawberry slices with sweetener, tossing gently until juice forms and coats berries. Set aside.

2. Grate 2 teaspoons rind from lemons. Squeeze lemons to measure ½ cup juice. Combine lemon rind, lemon juice, and milk, stirring until mixture thickens.

3. Spoon 2 tablespoons graham cracker crumbs into each of 6 (6-ounce) custard cups or small dessert bowls. Spoon about ¼ cup lemon mixture over crumbs in each dish; top evenly with strawberries. Serve immediately, or chill until ready to serve. Yield: 6 servings (serving size: 1 parfait).

Per serving: CALORIES 283 (2% from fat); FAT 0.5g (saturated fat 0g); PROTEIN 6g; CARBOHYDRATES 52.5g; FIBER 1.2g; CHOLESTEROL 8mg; IRON 0.5mg; SODIUM 21mg; CALCIUM 219mg

Strawberries with Mango Crème

prep: 14 minutes   *POINTS* value: 4

Crème de cacao, a dark, chocolate-flavored liqueur, gives this chilled dessert added richness. For a nonalcoholic version, substitute orange juice for the liqueur. Or for a mousselike consistency with the same *POINTS* value, fold ½ cup fat-free whipped topping into the mango crème.

   2   medium mangoes, peeled and cubed
  ¼   cup fat-free sweetened condensed milk
   2   tablespoons crème de cacao or fresh orange juice
  ½   teaspoon grated fresh lemon rind
  ½   teaspoon grated fresh orange rind
   4   cups quartered strawberries
   4   mint sprigs (optional)

1. Process first 5 ingredients in a blender until smooth.
2. Spoon mango crème into 4 dessert bowls; top with strawberries. Garnish with mint sprigs, if desired. Yield: 4 servings (serving size: about ⅓ cup mango crème and 1 cup strawberries).

Per serving: CALORIES 198 (5% from fat); FAT 1.1g (saturated fat 0g); PROTEIN 2.4g; CARBOHYDRATES 43.3g; FIBER 1.8g; CHOLESTEROL 3mg; IRON 0.6mg; SODIUM 22mg; CALCIUM 71mg

Grocery List

2 medium mangoes

1 small lemon

1 small orange

1 (16-ounce) package strawberries

1 small bunch fresh mint (optional)

1 (14-ounce) can fat-free sweetened condensed milk

1-liter bottle crème de cacao

Grocery List

1 medium navel orange

1 medium mango

1 (4.4-ounce) package blueberries

1 (16-ounce) package strawberries

1 small banana

1 (375-milliliter) bottle coffee-flavored liqueur (such as Kahlúa)

Five Fruit Medley

prep: 8 minutes

POINTS value: 1

A combination of fresh seasonal fruit makes a superquick dessert or a satisfying snack. For a little added flavor, we've tossed the fruit with Kahlúa, a coffee-flavored liqueur. If you prefer, simply omit the liqueur.

- 1 medium navel orange
- 2 teaspoons coffee-flavored liqueur (such as Kahlúa)
- 1 cup cubed mango
- ½ cup blueberries
- ¾ cup sliced strawberries
- ½ cup banana slices (about ½ small banana)

1. Peel and section orange over a medium bowl. Gently stir in liqueur and remaining fruit.
Yield: 6 servings (serving size: ½ cup).

Per serving: CALORIES 60 (3% from fat); FAT 0.3g (saturated fat 0g); PROTEIN 0.7g; CARBOHYDRATES 14.5g; FIBER 2g; CHOLESTEROL 0mg; IRON 0.2mg; SODIUM 1mg; CALCIUM 17mg

White Chocolate Panna Cotta

prep: 4 minutes • **cook:** 3 minutes • **other:** 8 hours   *POINTS* value: 5

Panna cotta is an Italian dessert made of heavy cream and served with either fresh berries, caramel topping, or chocolate sauce. We substituted fat-free half-and-half and fat-free sweetened condensed milk for the heavy cream and added a little white chocolate for flavor. Since this impressive dessert needs to chill 8 hours before serving, plan ahead so that you can serve it at your next dinner party.

 1 envelope unflavored gelatin
 2 cups fat-free half-and-half, divided
 3 ounces white chocolate, chopped
 1 cup fat-free sweetened condensed milk
 ½ teaspoon vanilla extract
 Raspberries (optional)

1. Sprinkle gelatin over 1 cup half-and-half in a small saucepan; let stand 1 to 2 minutes. Cook, stirring constantly, over medium heat 3 minutes or until gelatin dissolves; remove from heat. Add chocolate, stirring until it melts.

2. Gradually stir in remaining 1 cup half-and-half, condensed milk, and vanilla. Pour ½ cup custard into each of 6 stemmed glasses or 6-ounce custard cups. Cover and chill 8 hours. Serve with fresh berries, if desired. Yield: 6 servings (serving size: 1 panna cotta).

Per serving: CALORIES 281 (15% from fat); FAT 4.6g (saturated fat 2.8g); PROTEIN 5.8g; CARBOHYDRATES 48.4g; FIBER 0g; CHOLESTEROL 9mg; IRON 0.1mg; SODIUM 148mg; CALCIUM 216mg

Grocery List

1 (6-ounce) package raspberries (optional)

1 (1-ounce) package unflavored gelatin

1 (14-ounce) can fat-free sweetened condensed milk

1 (6-ounce) package white chocolate

1 (1-ounce) bottle vanilla extract

1 (16-ounce) carton fat-free half-and-half

Grocery List

8 small figs

1 small orange

1 (4-ounce) package chopped walnuts

1 (1.75-quart) container vanilla fat-free ice cream

Check staples: cooking spray and honey

Vanilla Ice Cream with Figs and Walnuts

prep: 9 minutes • **cook:** 10 minutes   *POINTS* value: 4

Warm, saucy fresh figs and toasted walnuts make a deliciously simple dessert. When figs are out of season, use fresh pears.

  8 small ripe figs, quartered
Cooking spray
  ¼ cup honey
  2 tablespoons fresh orange juice
  2 cups vanilla fat-free ice cream
  4 teaspoons chopped walnuts, toasted

1. Preheat oven to 400°.

2. Place figs in an 8-inch square baking dish coated with cooking spray. Combine honey and orange juice; pour over figs. Bake at 400° for 10 minutes or until figs are tender and golden brown.

3. Place ½ cup ice cream in each of 4 bowls. Spoon fig mixture evenly over ice cream and top evenly with walnuts. Serve immediately. Yield: 4 servings (serving size: ½ cup ice cream, 3 tablespoons fig mixture, and 1 teaspoon walnuts).

Per serving: CALORIES 191 (8% from fat); FAT 1.7g (saturated fat 0.2g); PROTEIN 3.7g; CARBOHYDRATES 42.1g; FIBER 1.9g; CHOLESTEROL 0mg; IRON 0.3mg; SODIUM 66mg; CALCIUM 113mg

pictured on page 48

Grilled Summer Fruit

prep: 3 minutes • **cook:** 6 minutes **POINTS** value: 2

If you're grilling chicken, fish, or beef for dinner, go ahead and grill your dessert as well. Serve with a dollop of reduced-fat sour cream or fat-free Greek-style yogurt.

1 medium lime
2 medium red plums, halved and pitted
1 medium nectarine, halved and pitted
2 (¾-inch-thick) cored fresh pineapple slices
1 tablespoon cinnamon sugar, divided
Butter-flavored cooking spray
¼ cup reduced-fat sour cream

1. Prepare grill.
2. Grate lime rind to measure ¼ teaspoon; set aside. Squeeze lime to measure 1 tablespoon juice. Brush plum halves, nectarine halves, and pineapple slices with juice. Sprinkle fruit with 1½ teaspoons cinnamon sugar; coat with cooking spray.
3. Grill fruit 3 minutes on each side or until fruit is hot and beginning to caramelize. Coarsely chop fruit. Combine fruit and grated lime rind; toss well. Divide warm fruit among 4 small dessert bowls. Top evenly with sour cream and sprinkle with remaining 1½ teaspoons cinnamon sugar. Serve immediately. Yield: 4 servings (serving size: ½ cup fruit and 1 tablespoon sour cream).

Per serving: CALORIES 87 (16% from fat); FAT 1.6g (saturated fat 1g); PROTEIN 1.8g; CARBOHYDRATES 18.2g; FIBER 1g; CHOLESTEROL 0mg; IRON 0.3mg; SODIUM 13mg; CALCIUM 6mg

Grocery List

1 medium lime

2 medium red plums

1 medium nectarine

1 peeled and cored pineapple

1 (3.6-ounce) jar cinnamon sugar

1 (8-ounce) carton reduced-fat sour cream

Check staples: butter-flavored cooking spray

Autumn Fruit Compote

prep: 5 minutes • **cook:** 4 hours, 30 minutes • **other:** 15 minutes *POINTS* value: 2

Serve this warm compote alone, topped with frozen yogurt or ice cream, or as a side dish to accompany roasted pork or ham.

   1 cup apple cider
   ¼ cup packed light brown sugar
   ¼ teaspoon ground cinnamon
   2 medium Golden Delicious apples, cored and cut into 8 wedges
   1 (7-ounce) package mixed dried fruit bits (such as Sun-Maid)

1. Combine first 3 ingredients in a 3-quart electric slow cooker, stirring until sugar dissolves. Arrange apple wedges in cider mixture; top with dried fruit. Cover and cook on LOW 4½ to 5 hours or until apples are tender. Let stand at least 15 minutes before serving. Yield: 8 servings (serving size: 2 apple wedges and ¼ cup fruit mixture).

Per serving: CALORIES 138 (0% from fat); FAT 0g (saturated fat 0g); PROTEIN 0.9g; CARBOHYDRATES 34.8g; FIBER 2.7g; CHOLESTEROL 0mg; IRON 0.7mg; SODIUM 16mg; CALCIUM 21mg

Goat Cheese and Asparagus Pizza, *page 91*

Mediterranean
Goat Cheese Spread,
page 12

Cranberry Citrus Spritzer, *page 21*

Arugula Salad with Prosciutto
and Pears, *page 154*

Mediterranean Cod, *page 66*

Chipotle-Yogurt Chicken
Kebabs, *page 134*

Ham and Butternut Squash
Soup, *page 185*

Chutney-Glazed Curry Pork
Tenderloin, *page 111*

Grilled Chicken and Tomato Pesto Baguettes, *page 172*

Pea, Carrot, and Tofu Salad,
page 153

Scallops with Lemon-Basil Sauce, *page 82*

Beef Tenderloin Steaks with
Mushroom Gravy, *page 103*

44

Creamy Chocolate-Hazelnut
Pie, *page 54*

Couscous Salad with
Roasted Chicken, *page 156*

Apricot-Honey-Nut Pound
Cake Panini, *page 62*

Grilled Summer Fruit,
page 31

Fresh Berry Crunch

prep: 5 minutes • **cook:** 1 minute   *POINTS* value: 3

A quick broil crisps this crumbled cookie topping and gives it a toasty flavor. If time is short, you can skip this step. To lower the *POINTS* value by 1, simply omit the sour cream.

  2 cups raspberries
  1 cup blueberries
  ¾ cup reduced-fat sour cream
  2 tablespoons turbinado sugar
  6 reduced-fat shortbread cookies (such as Keebler Sandies)

1. Preheat broiler.

2. Combine raspberries and blueberries in a bowl. Spoon ½ cup berries into each of 6 (6-ounce) custard cups or small dessert dishes. Top each serving with 2 tablespoons sour cream and 1 teaspoon sugar. Crumble 1 cookie over each custard cup.

3. Broil 1 minute or until cookie is golden. (Watch cookies closely when broiling; they brown fast). Yield: 6 servings (serving size: ½ cup berries, 2 tablespoons sour cream, 1 teaspoon sugar, and 1 cookie).

Per serving: CALORIES 165 (30% from fat); FAT 5.9g (saturated fat 2g); PROTEIN 2.7g; CARBOHYDRATES 27.5g; FIBER 3.3g; CHOLESTEROL 10mg; IRON 0.7mg; SODIUM 96mg; CALCIUM 12mg

Grocery List

1 (6-ounce) package raspberries

1 (4.4-ounce) package blueberries

1 (16-ounce) box turbinado sugar

1 (16-ounce) package reduced-fat shortbread cookies (such as Keebler Sandies)

1 (8-ounce) carton reduced-fat sour cream

Grocery List

4 large Granny Smith apples

1 small lemon

1 (18-ounce) box low-fat granola with raisins

1 (1-ounce) bottle vanilla extract

Check staples: butter-flavored cooking spray, brown sugar, and cornstarch

Apple-Granola Crisp

prep: 8 minutes • **cook:** 7 minutes

POINTS value: 3

To make this recipe even quicker, use a 1-pound bag of presliced apples. Look for it in the produce section at your supermarket.

 4 cups sliced Granny Smith apple (about 4 large apples)
 1 tablespoon brown sugar
 1 tablespoon cornstarch
 1 tablespoon lemon juice
 ½ teaspoon vanilla extract
 Butter-flavored cooking spray
 1¼ cups low-fat granola with raisins

1. Combine first 5 ingredients in a large bowl; toss well. Spoon mixture into an 11 x 7–inch baking dish coated with cooking spray. Cover with heavy-duty plastic wrap; microwave at HIGH 5 minutes or until apple is tender.

2. Remove plastic wrap. Top apple mixture with granola; coat generously with cooking spray. Microwave, uncovered, at HIGH 2 minutes. Yield: 4 servings (serving size: 1 cup).

Per serving: CALORIES 174 (9% from fat); FAT 1.7g (saturated fat 0.4g); PROTEIN 2.5g; CARBOHYDRATES 39.4g; FIBER 2.9g; CHOLESTEROL 0mg; IRON 0.8mg; SODIUM 70mg; CALCIUM 23mg

Warm Cherry Crisp

prep: 2 minutes • **cook:** 13 minutes   *POINTS* value: 5

In this recipe, low-fat granola saves you the time and effort of making the topping from scratch, and it delivers the same down-home result.

 1 (20-ounce) can light cherry pie filling
 ½ cup cherry-flavored sweetened dried cranberries
 2 tablespoons butter
 ½ teaspoon ground cinnamon
 ⅛ teaspoon salt
 Butter-flavored cooking spray
 2 cups low-fat granola

1. Preheat oven to 350°.
2. Combine first 5 ingredients in a medium saucepan; bring to a boil, stirring constantly, until butter melts.
3. Spoon cherry mixture into an 8-inch square baking dish coated with cooking spray. Sprinkle granola over cherry mixture. Spray top of granola with cooking spray. Bake at 350° for 10 minutes. Yield: 6 servings (serving size: about ½ cup).

Per serving: CALORIES 261 (20% from fat); FAT 5.9g (saturated fat 2.7g); PROTEIN 2.7g; CARBOHYDRATES 51.2g; FIBER 3.7g; CHOLESTEROL 10mg; IRON 1.3mg; SODIUM 172mg; CALCIUM 17mg

Grocery List

1 (6-ounce) package cherry-flavored sweetened dried cranberries

1 (18-ounce) box low-fat granola

1 (20-ounce) can light cherry pie filling

Check staples: butter, butter-flavored cooking spray, ground cinnamon, and salt

Grocery List

1 (10-ounce) round angel food cake

1 (2.25-ounce) package sliced almonds

1 (1-ounce) bottle almond extract

1 (20-ounce) can light cherry pie filling

1 (24-ounce) bottle chocolate syrup

1 (12-ounce) container frozen fat-free whipped topping

Chocolate-Cherry Trifle

prep: 7 minutes • **cook:** 2 minutes • **other:** 8 hours   *POINTS* value: 4

You can make this a day ahead and chill until ready to serve. Look for a prepared angel food cake in the bakery at your supermarket.

½   teaspoon almond extract
 1   (20-ounce) can light cherry pie filling
 1   (10-ounce) round angel food cake, torn into 2-inch pieces
½   cup chocolate syrup
 1   (12-ounce) container frozen fat-free whipped topping, thawed
 1   tablespoon sliced almonds, toasted

1. Stir almond extract into cherry pie filling. Place about 4 cups cake pieces in bottom of a 2½-quart trifle bowl; drizzle with ¼ cup chocolate syrup. Spread half of cherry pie filling over cake and chocolate syrup. Cover cherry pie filling with half of whipped topping. Repeat with remaining cake, chocolate syrup, cherry pie filling, and whipped topping. Sprinkle with almonds. Cover and chill at least 8 hours. Yield: 11 servings (serving size: 1 cup).

Per serving: CALORIES 194 (2% from fat); FAT 0.5g (saturated fat 0.1g); PROTEIN 2g; CARBOHYDRATES 43.1g; FIBER 1.1g; CHOLESTEROL 0mg; IRON 0.3mg; SODIUM 228mg; CALCIUM 37mg

pictured on page 113

Chocolate-Almond Ice Cream Cake

prep: 20 minutes • **other:** 1 hour, 30 minutes   ***POINTS*** value: **5**

Ice cream sandwiches are the key ingredient in this impressive dessert. We found that the rectangle sandwiches work best, so don't be tempted to use a round version. If you like the combination of chocolate and coconut, stir ¼ teaspoon coconut extract into the frozen whipped topping.

  2 (24-ounce) packages light triple-chocolate ice cream sandwiches (such as Blue Bunny)
  1 (12-ounce) container frozen fat-free whipped topping, thawed
 20 dark chocolate–covered almonds (such as Dove), coarsely chopped

1. Line a 9 x 5–inch loaf pan with foil. Arrange 4 ice cream sandwiches side by side on bottom of pan. Top with ⅔ cup whipped topping, and sprinkle with one-third of chopped almonds. Repeat layers once; top with ice cream sandwiches. Freeze 30 minutes or until firm.
2. Remove ice cream sandwich layers from loaf pan. Spread remaining whipped topping over top and sides of cake. Sprinkle remaining almonds on top. Cover and freeze at least 1 hour or until firm.
3. Cut evenly into 12 slices. Yield: 12 servings (serving size: 1 slice).

Per serving: CALORIES 250 (21% from fat); FAT 5.4g (saturated fat 2.8g); PROTEIN 4.4g; CARBOHYDRATES 42.5g; FIBER 0.9g; CHOLESTEROL 6mg; IRON 0.8mg; SODIUM 149mg; CALCIUM 105mg

Grocery List

2 (24-ounce) packages light triple-chocolate ice cream sandwiches (such as Blue Bunny)

1 (12-ounce) container frozen fat-free whipped topping

1 (4.5-ounce) package dark chocolate–covered almonds (such as Dove)

Grocery List

1 (13-ounce) jar chocolate-hazelnut spread (such as Nutella)

1 (1-ounce) package unflavored gelatin

1 (6-ounce) chocolate crumb piecrust

1 (14-ounce) container rolled wafer and hazelnut crème cookies (such as Crème de Pirouline; optional)

1 (16-ounce) bottle fat-free hazelnut liquid nondairy creamer

2 (8-ounce) blocks ⅓-less-fat cream cheese

1 (8-ounce) container frozen fat-free whipped topping (optional)

pictured on page 45

Creamy Chocolate-Hazelnut Pie

prep: 8 minutes • **cook:** 2 minutes • **other:** 12 hours   *POINTS* value: 7

For a smooth, creamy texture, be sure to allow the gelatin to dissolve completely before you add the cream cheese. Look for the chocolate-hazelnut spread alongside the peanut butter at your supermarket.

  2 teaspoons unflavored gelatin
  ¾ cup fat-free hazelnut liquid nondairy creamer, divided
  2 (8-ounce) blocks ⅓-less-fat cream cheese, softened
  ⅔ cup chocolate-hazelnut spread (such as Nutella)
  1 (6-ounce) chocolate crumb piecrust
  Frozen fat-free whipped topping (optional)
  Rolled wafer and hazelnut crème cookies (such as Crème de Pirouline; optional)

1. Sprinkle gelatin over ¼ cup creamer in a small saucepan; let stand 1 minute. Cook over low heat 2 minutes or until gelatin dissolves, stirring frequently.

2. Beat cream cheese with a mixer at medium speed until smooth. Add chocolate-hazelnut spread; beat well. Gradually add gelatin mixture and remaining ½ cup creamer, beating until smooth. Pour mixture into piecrust. Cover and chill 12 hours. Top each slice with whipped topping and a rolled wafer cookie, if desired. Yield: 12 servings (serving size: 1 slice).

Per serving: CALORIES 273 (53% from fat); FAT 16g (saturated fat 7.6g); PROTEIN 6.4g; CARBOHYDRATES 25.6g; FIBER 0.8g; CHOLESTEROL 27mg; IRON 0.6mg; SODIUM 250mg; CALCIUM 45mg

Frozen Coffee–Peanut Butter Ice Cream Pie

prep: 8 minutes • **cook:** 40 seconds • **other:** 4 hours   *POINTS* value: 5

Instant coffee granules add a depth of flavor to this frozen peanut butter pie.

- 4 cups vanilla fat-free ice cream
- ¼ cup reduced-fat peanut butter
- 1 (6-ounce) chocolate cookie piecrust (such as Oreo)
- 1 tablespoon instant coffee granules, divided

1. Microwave ice cream at HIGH 20 seconds or just until softened.

2. Place peanut butter in a small glass bowl and microwave at HIGH 20 seconds or until just melted. Spoon peanut butter into bottom of piecrust and spread evenly with the back of a spoon.

3. Spoon ice cream into a medium bowl; gently fold 2 teaspoons coffee granules into ice cream. Spoon ice cream into piecrust; cover and freeze at least 4 hours or until firm. Sprinkle pie with remaining 1 teaspoon coffee granules before serving. Yield: 8 servings (serving size: 1 slice).

Per serving: CALORIES 239 (28% from fat); FAT 7.6g (saturated fat 1.6g); PROTEIN 6g; CARBOHYDRATES 36.9g; FIBER 2g; CHOLESTEROL 0mg; IRON 0.5mg; SODIUM 239mg; CALCIUM 100mg

Grocery List

1 (18-ounce) jar reduced-fat peanut butter

1 (8-ounce) jar instant coffee granules

1 (6-ounce) chocolate cookie piecrust (such as Oreo)

1 (1.75-quart) container vanilla fat-free ice cream

Grocery List

2 medium peaches

1 (5.6-ounce) package blackberries

1 (6-ounce) package raspberries

1 (3.6-ounce) jar cinnamon sugar

1 (8-ounce) can refrigerated reduced-fat crescent dinner roll dough

1 (12-ounce) container frozen fat-free whipped topping (optional)

Check staples: butter-flavored cooking spray

Broiled Fruit Pizza

prep: 10 minutes • **cook:** 13 minutes   *POINTS* value: 3

Juicy summer peaches and fresh berries add a seasonal flair to this vibrantly colored dessert. Substitute nectarines for the peaches, if you prefer.

  1 (8-ounce) can refrigerated reduced-fat crescent dinner roll dough
Butter-flavored cooking spray
  2 medium peaches, peeled and cut into wedges
  1 cup blackberries
  1 cup raspberries
  2 tablespoons cinnamon sugar
Frozen fat-free whipped topping, thawed (optional)

1. Preheat oven to 425°.

2. Unroll dough, and separate into 8 triangles. Place triangles on a 12-inch pizza pan coated with cooking spray, skinny tips toward the center. Press dough triangles with hands to form a circle. Spray dough with cooking spray.

3. Bake at 425° for 8 minutes or until golden. Remove from oven and preheat broiler.

4. Top pizza evenly with fruit; sprinkle cinnamon sugar evenly over top. Broil 5 minutes or until fruit is tender and caramelized. Cut into 8 wedges and top with whipped topping, if desired. Yield: 8 servings (serving size: 1 wedge).

Per serving: CALORIES 141 (30% from fat); FAT 4.9g (saturated fat 1g); PROTEIN 2.7g; CARBOHYDRATES 22.4g; FIBER 2.7g; CHOLESTEROL 0mg; IRON 0.4mg; SODIUM 233mg; CALCIUM 13mg

Apple-Blueberry Turnovers

prep: 8 minutes • **cook:** 15 minutes

POINTS value: 4

Refrigerated pie dough simplifies the preparation, and light apple pie filling and fresh blueberries keep the *POINTS* value lower in these fruit turnovers. If you don't have a 6-inch round cutter, use a bowl or lid that has a 6-inch diameter. Use the tip of a sharp knife to cut the dough.

  1 (15-ounce) package refrigerated pie dough (such as Pillsbury)
  1 cup light apple pie filling, chopped
  ½ cup blueberries
  ½ teaspoon grated fresh lemon rind
  Cooking spray
  Powdered sugar (optional)

1. Preheat oven to 450°. Line a large baking sheet with parchment paper; set aside.

2. Roll dough into 2 (14-inch) circles. Using a 6-inch round cutter, cut each circle into 4 circles. Combine pie filling, blueberries, and lemon rind in a medium bowl, stirring well. Spread circles of dough evenly with pie filling mixture to within ¼ inch of edges. Fold crust over filling, pressing edges to seal.

3. Coat turnovers with cooking spray; place on prepared baking sheet. Bake at 450° for 15 minutes or until golden brown. Sprinkle with powdered sugar, if desired. Yield: 8 servings (serving size: 1 turnover).

Per serving: CALORIES 182 (45% from fat); FAT 9g (saturated fat 3.4g); PROTEIN 1.4g; CARBOHYDRATES 23.8g; FIBER 0.6g; CHOLESTEROL 6mg; IRON 0mg; SODIUM 134mg; CALCIUM 1mg

Grocery List

1 (4.4-ounce) package blueberries

1 small lemon

1 (20-ounce) can light apple pie filling

1 (15-ounce) package refrigerated pie dough (such as Pillsbury)

Check staples: cooking spray and powdered sugar (optional)

pictured on page 128

Cherry Turnovers

prep: 12 minutes • **cook:** 17 minutes

POINTS value: 5

We've baked instead of fried these flaky cherry-filled turnovers. The end result produced a restaurant-quality treat but with fewer calories and less fat.

Grocery List

1 (2-ounce) package slivered almonds

1 (20-ounce) can light cherry pie filling

1 (16-ounce) box turbinado sugar

1 (17.3-ounce) package frozen puff pastry

Check staples: eggs and cooking spray

½ (17.3-ounce) package frozen puff pastry, thawed
 1 (20-ounce) can light cherry pie filling, drained
 3 tablespoons slivered almonds, toasted and chopped
 1 large egg white, beaten
 1 tablespoon water
 2 tablespoons turbinado sugar
Cooking spray

1. Preheat oven to 400°.

2. Roll pastry sheet into a 12-inch square on a work surface. Cut into 9 (4-inch) squares. Divide cherry pie filling evenly among squares; sprinkle evenly with almonds. Whisk together egg white and water. Brush edges of pastry with egg mixture. Fold each square into a triangle, pressing edges to seal. Brush top of each pastry with remaining egg mixture, and sprinkle evenly with sugar. Place turnovers on a baking sheet coated with cooking spray.

3. Bake at 400° for 15 minutes or until golden. Yield: 9 servings (serving size: 1 turnover).

Per serving: CALORIES 212 (48% from fat); FAT 11.5g (saturated fat 2.7g); PROTEIN 2.9g; CARBOHYDRATES 24.9g; FIBER 1.3g; CHOLESTEROL 0mg; IRON 0.8mg; SODIUM 84mg; CALCIUM 9mg

pictured on page 126

Blackberry-Almond Cheesecake Tarts

prep: 7 minutes • **cook:** 5 minutes   *POINTS* value: 1

You'll love the contrasting textures of the crunchy phyllo shells and the velvety cream cheese mixture. To make the tarts ahead, prepare the filling and chill until you are ready to assemble.

 1 (2.1-ounce) package mini phyllo shells (such as Athens)
½ cup (4 ounces) ⅓-less-fat cream cheese
 1 tablespoon granulated sugar
 3 tablespoons vanilla fat-free yogurt
 1 teaspoon grated fresh lemon rind
⅛ teaspoon ground cinnamon
15 blackberries
 1 tablespoon sliced almonds
Powdered sugar for dusting

1. Preheat oven to 350°.

2. Toast phyllo shells at 350° for 5 minutes.

3. While phyllo shells cook, beat cream cheese in a small bowl with a mixer at medium speed until smooth. Add granulated sugar, yogurt, lemon rind, and cinnamon; beat at medium speed until combined.

4. Fill phyllo shells evenly with cream cheese mixture. Top evenly with blackberries and almonds. Dust with powdered sugar; serve immediately. Yield: 15 servings (serving size: 1 tart).

Per serving: CALORIES 50 (52% from fat); FAT 2.9g (saturated fat 1.1g); PROTEIN 1.2g; CARBOHYDRATES 5.1g; FIBER 0.6g; CHOLESTEROL 5mg; IRON 0.3mg; SODIUM 48mg; CALCIUM 15mg

Grocery List

1 small lemon

1 (5.6-ounce) package blackberries

1 (2.25-ounce) package sliced almonds

1 (8-ounce) block ⅓-less-fat cream cheese

1 (6-ounce) carton vanilla fat-free yogurt

1 (2.1-ounce) package mini phyllo shells (such as Athens)

Check staples: granulated sugar, powdered sugar, and ground cinnamon

Grocery List

1 medium mango

1 medium kiwi

1 (10-ounce) jar apricot fruit spread

1 (4-ounce) package miniature graham cracker piecrusts

1 (7-ounce) package flaked sweetened coconut

1 (8-ounce) carton vanilla fat-free yogurt

Individual Mango-Kiwi Tarts

prep: 13 minutes • **cook:** 2 minutes, 30 seconds   *POINTS* value: 5

We prefer fresh mango, but the refrigerated jarred version will work, too. To toast coconut, place a skillet over medium heat until hot. Add the coconut and cook 2 minutes or until lightly golden and fragrant, stirring frequently.

- 6 tablespoons apricot fruit spread
- 6 miniature graham cracker piecrusts
- 1 cup vanilla fat-free yogurt
- 1 medium mango, peeled and diced
- 1 medium kiwi, peeled and diced
- 3 tablespoons flaked sweetened coconut, lightly toasted

1. Place fruit spread in a small microwave-safe bowl; microwave at HIGH 30 seconds or until melted.

2. Spoon 1 tablespoon melted fruit spread into each piecrust. Top with equal amounts of yogurt, mango, kiwi, and coconut. Yield: 6 servings (serving size: 1 tart).

Per serving: CALORIES 239 (26% from fat); FAT 6.9g (saturated fat 1.7g); PROTEIN 3.5g; CARBOHYDRATES 41.4g; FIBER 2.3g; CHOLESTEROL 1mg; IRON 0.5mg; SODIUM 186mg; CALCIUM 81mg

Sweet and Creamy Pumpkin Mini Pies

prep: 15 minutes

POINTS value: 4

The two main ingredients in this easy dessert, canned pumpkin and light cream cheese, mean there's no baking required. Freeze any extra mini pies for a tasty frozen treat.

½ (15-ounce) can unsweetened pumpkin
¼ cup "measures-like-sugar" sweetener (such as Splenda)
⅛ cup (1 ounce) tub-style light cream cheese, softened
 1 teaspoon vanilla extract
½ teaspoon pumpkin-pie spice
⅛ teaspoon salt
½ (8-ounce) container frozen fat-free whipped topping, thawed
 6 miniature graham cracker piecrusts
Frozen fat-free whipped topping, thawed (optional)
Pumpkin-pie spice (optional)

1. Combine first 6 ingredients in a medium bowl. Add ½ (8-ounce) container whipped topping, and stir gently until blended.

2. Spoon equal amounts of pumpkin mixture into each piecrust. Top each with whipped topping, and sprinkle lightly with pumpkin-pie spice, if desired. Chill until ready to serve. Yield: 6 servings (serving size: 1 pie).

Per serving: CALORIES 216 (29% from fat); FAT 6.9g (saturated fat 1.6g); PROTEIN 1.8g; CARBOHYDRATES 27.9g; FIBER 2.1g; CHOLESTEROL 2mg; IRON 0.9mg; SODIUM 330mg; CALCIUM 16mg

Grocery List

1 (15-ounce) can unsweetened pumpkin

1 (1-ounce) bottle vanilla extract

1 (1.12-ounce) jar pumpkin-pie spice

1 (4-ounce) package miniature graham cracker piecrusts

1 (8-ounce) tub light cream cheese

1 (8-ounce) container frozen fat-free whipped topping

Check staples: "measures-like-sugar" sweetener (such as Splenda) and salt

pictured on page 47

Apricot-Honey-Nut Pound Cake Panini

prep: 7 minutes • **cook:** 4 minutes • **other:** 2 minutes   *POINTS* value: 4

A panini press is the ideal appliance to use for this dessert, but we found a table-top electric grill worked just as well. If you have neither, cook 3 minutes on each side in a nonstick skillet over medium heat.

  1 (10-ounce) loaf frozen low-fat pound cake (such as Sara Lee), thawed
 ⅓ cup (2.6 ounces) tub-style light cream cheese
 ¼ cup chopped dried apricots
  1 tablespoon honey
  1 tablespoon chopped natural almonds
Butter-flavored cooking spray

1. Slice pound cake into 12 equal slices. Combine cream cheese and apricots, stirring well. Spread a rounded tablespoonful cream cheese mixture onto each of 6 slices pound cake; drizzle ½ teaspoon honey over each slice topped with cream cheese mixture. Sprinkle chopped almonds evenly over honey. Top with remaining 6 pound cake slices. Coat exposed cake slices with cooking spray.

2. Cook panini, in 2 batches, in preheated panini press or tabletop grill 2 to 3 minutes or until golden and toasted. Let stand 2 to 3 minutes before serving. Yield: 6 servings (serving size: 1 panini).

Per serving: CALORIES 200 (25% from fat); FAT 5.5g (saturated fat 2.3g); PROTEIN 3.8g; CARBOHYDRATES 34.1g; FIBER 1.1g; CHOLESTEROL 7mg; IRON 2.7mg; SODIUM 260mg; CALCIUM 37mg

Lemon Gingersnap Cookie Sandwiches

prep: 15 minutes • **cook:** 2 minutes

POINTS value: 3

Make these sandwich cookies to keep on hand and store in the refrigerator for a quick snack or dessert. Their texture will soften to resemble ice cream sandwiches.

½ cup (4 ounces) ⅓-less-fat cream cheese
¼ cup powdered sugar
1 teaspoon grated fresh lemon rind
20 gingersnaps
3 tablespoons slivered almonds, toasted and chopped

1. Combine first 3 ingredients in a small bowl; stir until smooth. Spoon 1 tablespoon cream cheese mixture on 1 cookie; top with another cookie, and gently press until cream cheese mixture reaches edges. Carefully smooth filling around edge of sandwich with a spatula. Roll edge of sandwich in chopped almonds. Repeat with remaining cookies. Serve immediately, or wrap each sandwich in plastic wrap and store in refrigerator until ready to serve. Yield: 10 servings (serving size: 1 sandwich).

Per serving: CALORIES 111 (40% from fat); FAT 4.9g (saturated fat 2.1g); PROTEIN 2.4g; CARBOHYDRATES 14.7g; FIBER 0.6g; CHOLESTEROL 8mg; IRON 1mg; SODIUM 143mg; CALCIUM 24mg

Grocery List

1 small lemon

1 (2-ounce) package slivered almonds

1 (16-ounce) package gingersnaps

1 (8-ounce) block ⅓-less-fat cream cheese

Check staples: powdered sugar

Gooey Peanut Butter S'mores

prep: 5 minutes • **cook:** 1 minute   *POINTS* value: 3

You don't need a campfire to make these yummy s'mores. You can use a baking sheet and your oven's broiler to toast the marshmallows.

  6   sheets low-fat graham crackers, split in half
  6   large marshmallows
  6   teaspoons fat-free hot fudge topping, divided
 ¼   cup reduced-fat peanut butter

1. Preheat broiler.

2. Place 6 graham cracker halves on a baking sheet; top each with 1 marshmallow. Broil 1 minute or until toasted. Drizzle 1 teaspoon hot fudge topping over each marshmallow.

3. Spread 2 teaspoons peanut butter on each remaining graham cracker half. Place on top of toasted marshmallows, peanut butter sides down, and press gently. Serve immediately. Yield: 6 servings (serving size: 1 s'more).

Per serving: CALORIES 158 (27% from fat); FAT 4.8g (saturated fat 0.8g); PROTEIN 3.7g; CARBOHYDRATES 26g; FIBER 1.2g; CHOLESTEROL 0mg; IRON 0.8mg; SODIUM 187mg; CALCIUM 75mg

Fish & Shellfish

pictured on page 37

Mediterranean Cod

prep: 3 minutes • **cook:** 4 minutes   **POINTS** value: 5

The oil-packed sun-dried tomatoes pull double duty in this recipe. The aromatic oil infuses the fish with rich, vibrant flavor, while the sun-dried tomatoes add color and texture to the topping. Bring the water for the couscous to a boil while you chop the other ingredients. Cook the fish while the couscous stands.

Grocery List

1 small bunch fresh parsley

1 (7-ounce) jar oil-packed sun-dried tomato halves

1 small red onion

1 (5- or 6-ounce) package fresh baby spinach

1 (7-ounce) jar pitted kalamata olives

1 (10-ounce) box uncooked plain couscous

4 (6-ounce) cod fillets (about 1¼ inches thick)

Check staples: salt and black pepper

  2 tablespoons chopped fresh parsley
  4 oil-packed sun-dried tomato halves, drained and finely chopped
  6 pitted kalamata olives, chopped
  4 teaspoons oil from oil-packed sun-dried tomatoes, divided
  4 (6-ounce) cod fillets (about 1¼ inches thick)
  ¼ teaspoon salt
  ¼ teaspoon freshly ground black pepper

1. Combine first 3 ingredients and 1 teaspoon sun-dried tomato oil in a small bowl; set aside. Sprinkle fish with salt and pepper.

2. Heat remaining 1 tablespoon sun-dried tomato oil in a large nonstick skillet over medium-high heat. Add fish to pan, and cook 2 to 3 minutes on each side or until fish flakes easily when tested with a fork. Transfer fish to a serving platter; top evenly with tomato mixture. Serve immediately. Yield: 4 servings (serving size: 1 fillet and about 1½ table-spoons tomato mixture).

Per serving: CALORIES 203 (34% from fat); FAT 7.7g (saturated fat 1.1g); PROTEIN 30.6g; CARBOHYDRATES 1.4g; FIBER 0.3g; CHOLESTEROL 73mg; IRON 0.9mg; SODIUM 338mg; CALCIUM 34mg

Spinach and Onion Couscous

prep: 2 minutes • **cook:** 4 minutes • **other:** 5 minutes   **POINTS** value: 1

Combine ¾ cup water, ¼ cup finely chopped red onion, and ¼ teaspoon salt in a medium microwave-safe bowl. Cover bowl with heavy-duty plastic wrap, and vent. Microwave at HIGH 2 minutes. Coarsely chop 1 (5- or 6-ounce) package fresh baby spinach. Add spinach and ½ cup uncooked couscous to water mixture; cover and microwave at HIGH 2 minutes. Let stand, covered, 5 minutes; fluff with a fork. Serve immediately. Yield: 4 servings (serving size: ¾ cup).

Per serving: CALORIES 103 (1% from fat); FAT 0.2g (saturated fat 0g); PROTEIN 3.9g; CARBOHYDRATES 22.2g; FIBER 3.3g; CHOLESTEROL 0mg; IRON 1.6mg; SODIUM 215mg; CALCIUM 38mg

Apricot-Glazed Flounder

prep: 3 minutes • **cook:** 8 minutes   ***POINTS* value: 5**

Quickly thaw the frozen fish in the microwave at 30% power for 5 to 6 minutes. Be careful not to overheat the fish because it will begin to cook. Substitute peach or pineapple preserves for the apricot preserves, if you'd like.

```
    Cooking spray
 4  (3-ounce) frozen flounder fillets, thawed
¼   teaspoon salt
¼   teaspoon freshly ground black pepper
¼   cup reduced-sugar apricot preserves
 3  tablespoons water
 1  teaspoon low-sodium soy sauce
¼   teaspoon grated peeled fresh ginger
```

1. Heat a large nonstick skillet over medium-high heat. Generously coat pan with cooking spray. Sprinkle fish with salt and pepper. Add 2 fillets to pan; cook 2 minutes on each side or until fish flakes easily when tested with a fork. Remove fish from pan; keep warm. Repeat with remaining fillets.

2. Reduce heat to medium. Add apricot preserves and next 3 ingredients to pan. Cook 30 seconds or until hot. Pour glaze over fish, and serve immediately. Yield: 2 servings (serving size: 2 fillets and about ¼ cup glaze).

Per serving: CALORIES 248 (25% from fat); FAT 6.7g (saturated fat 1.2g); PROTEIN 32.3g; CARBOHYDRATES 12.4g; FIBER 0.1g; CHOLESTEROL 82mg; IRON 0.6mg; SODIUM 529mg; CALCIUM 32mg

Garden Salad

prep: 2 minutes   ***POINTS* value: 2**

Combine 3 cups sweet baby greens (such as Fresh Express); ½ small red bell pepper, cut into thin strips; and 2 thinly sliced green onions in a medium bowl. Drizzle with 3 tablespoons light honey Dijon dressing (such as Good Seasons); toss well, and sprinkle with freshly ground black pepper. Yield: 2 servings (serving size: 1¾ cups).

Per serving: CALORIES 92 (40% from fat); FAT 4.1g (saturated fat 0.4g); PROTEIN 7.6g; CARBOHYDRATES 12.3g; FIBER 2.7g; CHOLESTEROL 4mg; IRON 1.3mg; SODIUM 167mg; CALCIUM 52mg

Menu
***POINTS* value: 7**

Apricot-Glazed Flounder
Garden Salad

Grocery List

1 small piece ginger

1 (5-ounce) package sweet baby greens (such as Fresh Express)

1 small red bell pepper

1 small bunch green onions

1 (10-ounce) jar reduced-sugar apricot preserves

1 (10-ounce) bottle low-sodium soy sauce

1 (14-ounce) bottle light honey Dijon dressing (such as Good Seasons)

1 (12-ounce) package frozen flounder fillets

Check staples: cooking spray, salt, and black pepper

Menu

POINTS value: 9

Crab-Stuffed Flounder

Lemon-Scented Rice Pilaf

¾ cup steamed
green beans ☑.
POINTS value: 0

Grocery List

1 large shallot

1 or 2 small lemons

1 small red bell pepper

1 small bunch green onions

1 (12-ounce) package pretrimmed green beans

1 (24-ounce) loaf light whole wheat bread

1 (8.8-ounce) package precooked long-grain white rice (such as Uncle Ben's)

1 (16-ounce) container fresh lump crabmeat

4 (6-ounce) flounder fillets

Check staples: butter, olive oil, cooking spray, salt, and black pepper

Crab-Stuffed Flounder

prep: 4 minutes • **cook:** 18 minutes   *POINTS* value: 6

Plan to use the extra crabmeat to make the Crab Melts on page 161.

  1 (0.8-ounce) slice light whole wheat bread
  4 ounces fresh lump crabmeat, shell pieces removed (about ⅔ cup)
  ¼ teaspoon black pepper, divided
  2 teaspoons butter, divided
  ¼ cup finely chopped shallots (about 1 large)
  4 (6-ounce) flounder fillets
  ¼ teaspoon salt
Cooking spray
Lemon wedges (optional)

1. Preheat oven to 450°.

2. Place bread in a blender or mini food processor; pulse 10 times or until coarse crumbs measure ½ cup. Combine breadcrumbs, crabmeat, and ⅛ teaspoon pepper in a bowl.

3. Heat ½ teaspoon butter in a small nonstick skillet over medium heat. Add shallots, and cook 3 to 4 minutes or until tender. Add shallots to breadcrumb mixture, and toss gently.

4. Sprinkle fish evenly with salt and remaining ⅛ teaspoon pepper. Place one-fourth of crab mixture onto widest part of each fillet. Carefully roll up jelly-roll fashion; place fish, seam sides down, in a baking dish coated with cooking spray. Bake at 450° for 15 to 18 minutes or until fish flakes easily when tested with a fork.

5. Microwave remaining 1½ teaspoons butter at HIGH 20 seconds or until butter melts; drizzle over cooked fish. Serve with lemon wedges, if desired. Yield: 4 servings (serving size: 1 fillet).

Per serving: CALORIES 311 (14% from fat); FAT 4.9g (saturated fat 1.7g); PROTEIN 43.7g; CARBOHYDRATES 24.7g; FIBER 8.9g; CHOLESTEROL 108mg; IRON 2.7mg; SODIUM 709mg; CALCIUM 102mg

Lemon-Scented Rice Pilaf

prep: 5 minutes • **cook:** 3 minutes   *POINTS* value: 3

Heat 1 teaspoon olive oil in a small nonstick skillet coated with cooking spray over medium-high heat. Add ½ cup chopped red bell pepper and ¼ cup chopped green onions; sauté 2 minutes or until tender. Heat 1 (8.8-ounce) package precooked long-grain white rice (such as Uncle Ben's) in the microwave according to package directions. Stir in red bell pepper mixture, 1 tablespoon grated lemon rind, and ¼ teaspoon salt. Yield: 4 servings (serving size: ½ cup).

Per serving: CALORIES 140 (10% from fat); FAT 1.5g (saturated fat 0.3g); PROTEIN 2.8g; CARBOHYDRATES 28.4g; FIBER 1g; CHOLESTEROL 0mg; IRON 1.3mg; SODIUM 148mg; CALCIUM 17mg

Pan-Seared Grouper with Wilted Greens ☑

prep: 2 minutes • **cook:** 9 minutes   *POINTS* value: 4

Place the tomatoes in the oven to roast before preparing the fish so that they'll be ready to serve at the same time.

 1 tablespoon olive oil, divided
 4 (6-ounce) grouper fillets (about 1 inch thick)
 1 teaspoon freshly ground black pepper, divided
 ½ teaspoon salt, divided
 1 (5- or 6-ounce) package fresh baby spinach
 1 (4-ounce) bag organic herb mix salad
 1 tablespoon balsamic vinegar
 4 lemon wedges

1. Heat 2 teaspoons oil in a large nonstick skillet over medium-high heat. Sprinkle fish with ½ teaspoon pepper and ¼ teaspoon salt. Add fish to pan; cook 3 to 4 minutes on each side or until fish flakes easily when tested with a fork. Remove fish from pan; keep warm.
2. Add remaining 1 teaspoon oil to pan, and heat over medium-high heat. Add baby spinach, herb mix salad, vinegar, and remaining ½ teaspoon pepper and ¼ teaspoon salt; cook 30 seconds or just until greens begin to wilt. Divide greens evenly among 4 plates; top with fish and any accumulated juices. Serve with lemon wedges. Yield: 4 servings (serving size: 1 fillet and about ½ cup greens).

Per serving: CALORIES 218 (22% from fat); FAT 5.3g (saturated fat 0.9g); PROTEIN 34.8g; CARBOHYDRATES 8.1g; FIBER 3.4g; CHOLESTEROL 63mg; IRON 4.3mg; SODIUM 476mg; CALCIUM 113mg

Roasted Tomatoes

prep: 3 minutes • **cook:** 12 minutes   *POINTS* value: 1

Preheat oven to 500°. Cut 2 large tomatoes in half horizontally, and place on a broiler pan. Sprinkle cut sides of tomato evenly with ¼ teaspoon salt and ¼ teaspoon freshly ground black pepper; top evenly with ¼ cup torn fresh basil and ¼ cup (1 ounce) shredded part-skim mozzarella cheese. Bake at 500° for 12 minutes or until cheese melts and is lightly browned. Yield: 4 servings (serving size: 1 tomato half).

Per serving: CALORIES 39 (37% from fat); FAT 1.6g (saturated fat 0.9g); PROTEIN 2.7g; CARBOHYDRATES 4g; FIBER 1.2g; CHOLESTEROL 4mg; IRON 0.4mg; SODIUM 187mg; CALCIUM 65mg

Menu

POINTS value: 7

Pan-Seared Grouper with Wilted Greens

Roasted Tomatoes

1 (1.3-ounce) dinner roll
POINTS value: 2

Grocery List

1 (5- or 6-ounce) package fresh baby spinach

1 (4-ounce) bag organic herb mix salad

1 small lemon

2 large tomatoes

1 small bunch fresh basil

1 (1-pound) package dinner rolls (such as Arnold)

1 (4-ounce) package shredded part-skim mozzarella cheese

4 (6-ounce) grouper fillets (about 1 inch thick)

Check staples: olive oil, balsamic vinegar, salt, and black pepper

Grocery List

1 medium onion

1 small bunch fresh thyme

1 small bunch fresh mint

1 small lemon

1 medium shallot

6 very thin slices prosciutto or
ham (about 2 ounces)

1 (750-milliliter) bottle dry
white wine

1 (16-ounce) package frozen
petite green peas

4 (6-ounce) grouper fillets

Check staples: cooking spray,
salt, and black pepper

Grouper with Onions and Prosciutto

prep: 4 minutes • **cook:** 18 minutes   **POINTS value: 4**

Prosciutto, a salt-cured ham, balances the sweetness from the white wine and elevates the flavor in this succulent fish dish. Look for prosciutto in the deli section at your supermarket. We recommend using a dry white wine for this recipe, but you can use fat-free, less-sodium chicken broth instead.

Cooking spray
4 (6-ounce) grouper fillets
¼ teaspoon salt
¼ teaspoon freshly ground black pepper
1 cup thinly sliced onion
6 very thin slices prosciutto or ham, cut crosswise into thin strips (about 2 ounces)
¾ cup dry white wine
1 teaspoon minced fresh thyme

1. Heat a large nonstick skillet over medium-high heat. Coat pan with cooking spray. Sprinkle fish with salt and pepper. Add fish to pan; cook 2 to 3 minutes on each side or until browned. Remove from pan.

2. Add onion and prosciutto to pan; cook 3 minutes. Add wine, and bring to a boil. Return fish to pan; cover, reduce heat to low, and simmer 6 to 8 minutes.

3. Add thyme to pan; bring mixture to a boil. Cook, uncovered, 2 minutes or until liquid is slightly reduced and fish flakes easily when tested with a fork. Yield: 4 servings (serving size: 1 fillet and about 3 tablespoons sauce).

Per serving: CALORIES 202 (15% from fat); FAT 3.3g (saturated fat 0.9g); PROTEIN 37.4g; CARBOHYDRATES 4g; FIBER 0.6g; CHOLESTEROL 71mg; IRON 2mg; SODIUM 493mg; CALCIUM 57mg

Minted Pea Salad ✓.

prep: 7 minutes   **POINTS value: 2**

Place 4 cups frozen petite green peas in a colander, and rinse under cool running water to thaw; drain well. Grate 1 teaspoon rind from 1 lemon. Squeeze lemon to measure 1 teaspoon juice; reserve remaining lemon for another use. Combine peas, ½ cup torn fresh mint leaves, and 1 thinly sliced shallot in a medium bowl. Add lemon rind, lemon juice, ¼ teaspoon salt, and ⅛ teaspoon black pepper; toss gently to combine. Yield: 4 servings (serving size: 1 cup).

Per serving: CALORIES 120 (4% from fat); FAT 0.6g (saturated fat 0.1g); PROTEIN 8g; CARBOHYDRATES 22g; FIBER 6.4g; CHOLESTEROL 0mg; IRON 2.5mg; SODIUM 308mg; CALCIUM 41mg

Olive Pesto–Crusted Fish

prep: 4 minutes • **cook:** 12 minutes   *POINTS* value: 5

This simple recipe uses green olives and pesto to deliver bold flavor. Substitute snapper or halibut for the grouper, if desired.

¾ cup panko (Japanese breadcrumbs)
⅓ cup chopped pitted green olives
2 tablespoons commercial pesto
4 (6-ounce) grouper fillets
Cooking spray

1. Preheat oven to 400°.
2. Combine first 3 ingredients in a small bowl.
3. Place fish on a baking sheet coated with cooking spray. Press breadcrumb mixture evenly on top of fish. Bake at 400° for 12 minutes or until fish flakes easily when tested with a fork. Yield: 4 servings (serving size: 1 fillet).

Per serving: CALORIES 251 (25% from fat); FAT 6.9g (saturated fat 1g); PROTEIN 35.3g; CARBOHYDRATES 8.9g; FIBER 0.6g; CHOLESTEROL 65mg; IRON 1.7mg; SODIUM 341mg; CALCIUM 65mg

Sautéed Asparagus with Red Bell Pepper ☑

prep: 3 minutes • **cook:** 7 minutes   *POINTS* value: 1

Heat 2 teaspoons olive oil in a large nonstick skillet over medium-high heat; add 1 pound asparagus spears, trimmed, and 1 medium red bell pepper, thinly sliced. Sauté 6 minutes or until vegetables are crisp-tender. Add 1 minced garlic clove; sauté 1 minute. Remove from heat, and sprinkle with 1 tablespoon chopped fresh basil, ¼ teaspoon salt, and ⅛ teaspoon black pepper. Yield: 4 servings (serving size: about ¾ cup).

Per serving: CALORIES 54 (36% from fat); FAT 2.4g (saturated fat 0.4g); PROTEIN 2.8g; CARBOHYDRATES 7g; FIBER 3.1g; CHOLESTEROL 0mg; IRON 0.6mg; SODIUM 147mg; CALCIUM 29mg

Menu

POINTS value: 8

Olive Pesto–Crusted Fish

Sautéed Asparagus with Red Bell Pepper

½ cup lemon sorbet
POINTS value: 2

Grocery List

1 pound asparagus spears

1 medium red bell pepper

1 whole garlic head

1 small bunch fresh basil

1 (7-ounce) jar pitted green olives

1 (10-ounce) jar commercial pesto

1 (9-ounce) container panko (Japanese breadcrumbs)

1 pint lemon sorbet

4 (6-ounce) grouper fillets

Check staples: olive oil, cooking spray, salt, and black pepper

Red Curry Mahimahi

Coconut-Pineapple-Ginger Rice

½ cup steamed
sugar snap peas ☑.
POINTS value: 0

Grocery List

1 or 2 medium limes

1 small piece ginger

1 small bunch fresh cilantro

1 (8-ounce) package sugar snap peas

1 (2.25-ounce) package sliced almonds

1 (8-ounce) can pineapple tidbits in juice

1 (4-ounce) jar red curry paste

1 (13.5-ounce) can light coconut milk

1 (14-ounce) box boil-in-bag jasmine rice

1 (9-ounce) container panko (Japanese breadcrumbs)

4 (6-ounce) mahimahi fillets

Check staples: butter-flavored cooking spray and salt

Red Curry Mahimahi

prep: 9 minutes • **cook:** 9 minutes   *POINTS* value: 4

Look for panko, Japanese breadcrumbs, alongside the baking ingredients at your supermarket. These light, crispy breadcrumbs give the fish a delicate crust.

  1 tablespoon fresh lime juice
1½ teaspoons red curry paste
  3 tablespoons panko (Japanese breadcrumbs)
  3 tablespoons sliced almonds, chopped
  4 (6-ounce) mahimahi fillets
¼ teaspoon salt
    Butter-flavored cooking spray
    Lime wedges (optional)

1. Preheat oven to 450°.

2. Combine lime juice and curry paste in a small bowl. Combine breadcrumbs and almonds in a small bowl; set aside.

3. Pat fish dry with a paper towel. Place fish on a jelly-roll pan lined with foil. Sprinkle fillets evenly with salt; brush with lime juice mixture. Press breadcrumb mixture evenly on top of fish; spray with cooking spray.

4. Bake 9 to 10 minutes or until crust is browned and fish flakes easily when tested with a fork. Serve with lime wedges, if desired. Yield: 4 servings (serving size: 1 fillet).

Per serving: CALORIES 184 (17% from fat); FAT 3.5g (saturated fat 0.5g); PROTEIN 32.8g; CARBOHYDRATES 3.3g; FIBER 0.6g; CHOLESTEROL 124mg; IRON 1.9mg; SODIUM 337mg; CALCIUM 38mg

Coconut-Pineapple-Ginger Rice

prep: 4 minutes • **cook:** 12 minutes   *POINTS* value: 2

Drain 1 (8-ounce) can pineapple tidbits in juice, reserving juice. Combine pineapple juice, 3¾ cups water, and 1 (3.5-ounce) package boil-in-bag jasmine rice in a saucepan. Bring to a boil; boil, uncovered, 8 minutes. Drain well. While rice cooks, heat a large nonstick skillet over medium-high heat. Coat pan with butter-flavored cooking spray. Add 1 tablespoon minced peeled fresh ginger and drained pineapple tidbits; sauté 4 minutes or until caramelized. Combine ginger mixture, rice, 1 tablespoon chopped fresh cilantro, 2 tablespoons light coconut milk, and ¼ teaspoon salt. Serve immediately. Yield: 4 servings (serving size: ½ cup).

Per serving: CALORIES 122 (3% from fat); FAT 0.4g (saturated fat 0.4g); PROTEIN 2g; CARBOHYDRATES 29.3g; FIBER 0.5g; CHOLESTEROL 0mg; IRON 1mg; SODIUM 148mg; CALCIUM 8mg

Orange Roughy with Bacon and Leeks

prep: 9 minutes • **cook:** 14 minutes   *POINTS* value: 3

Cooking the fish and vegetables in foil packets traps the steam inside, keeping the fish moist and the vegetables tender. Cleanup is easy, too.

- ½   cup matchstick-cut carrots
- ½   cup thinly sliced leek
- 4   (6-ounce) orange roughy fillets
- 1   teaspoon dried tarragon
- ½   teaspoon salt
- ¼   teaspoon freshly ground black pepper
- 2   lower-sodium bacon slices, cooked and crumbled
- Olive oil–flavored cooking spray

1. Preheat oven to 475°. Place a baking sheet in oven while preheating.

2. Cut 4 (12-inch) squares of foil. Spoon carrot and leek evenly into center of each foil square; top each with a fish fillet. Sprinkle fish evenly with tarragon, salt, pepper, and crumbled bacon. Coat each fillet with cooking spray. Fold foil over fillets to make packets, and seal edges tightly.

3. Place packets on hot baking sheet. Bake at 475° for 14 minutes. Transfer fish and vegetables to serving plates, and serve immediately. Yield: 4 servings (serving size: 1 fillet and ¼ cup vegetables).

Per serving: CALORIES 158 (13% from fat); FAT 2.3g (saturated fat 0.4g); PROTEIN 29.3g; CARBOHYDRATES 3.3g; FIBER 0.7g; CHOLESTEROL 105mg; IRON 2.2mg; SODIUM 469mg; CALCIUM 33mg

Rustic Mashed Red Potatoes

prep: 3 minutes • **cook:** 8 minutes   *POINTS* value: 2

Place 1 pound small red potatoes in a medium microwave-safe bowl; cover tightly with plastic wrap. Microwave at HIGH 8 minutes or until potatoes are fork-tender. Add ¼ cup fat-free milk, 1 tablespoon light stick butter, and ¼ teaspoon each salt, garlic powder, and black pepper. Mash to desired consistency with a potato masher or fork. Yield: 4 servings (serving size: about ½ cup).

Per serving: CALORIES 98 (13% from fat); FAT 1.4g (saturated fat 0.6g); PROTEIN 2.7g; CARBOHYDRATES 19g; FIBER 2g; CHOLESTEROL 2mg; IRON 0.9mg; SODIUM 182mg; CALCIUM 31mg

Menu

POINTS value: 6

Orange Roughy with Bacon and Leeks

Rustic Mashed Red Potatoes

½ cup steamed haricots verts or baby green beans ✔.
POINTS value: 1

Grocery List

1 (10-ounce) package matchstick-cut carrots

1 small leek

1 pound small red potatoes

1 (8-ounce) package haricots verts or baby green beans

1 (1-pound) package lower-sodium bacon slices

4 (6-ounce) orange roughy fillets

Check staples: light stick butter, fat-free milk, olive oil–flavored cooking spray, dried tarragon, garlic powder, salt, and black pepper

Menu

POINTS value: 7

Orange Roughy with Lemon and Capers

Sautéed Corn and Tomatoes

1 (1-ounce) slice focaccia
POINTS value: 3

Grocery List

1 large lemon

1 small bunch fresh thyme

1 small bunch fresh basil

1 (1-pound) container grape tomatoes

1 whole garlic head

1 (12-ounce) focaccia loaf

1 (3.5-ounce) jar capers

1 (10-ounce) package frozen whole-kernel corn

4 (6-ounce) orange roughy fillets

Check staples: cooking spray, salt, and black pepper

Orange Roughy with Lemon and Capers ✔

prep: 5 minutes • **cook:** 15 minutes   **POINTS value: 3**

This Mediterranean-style dish relies on the sharp, salty taste of capers to provide its assertive flavor. Serve with a warm slice of focaccia from your supermarket's bakery to soak up the savory cooking juices.

  4 (6-ounce) orange roughy fillets
  4 teaspoons fresh lemon juice
  2 tablespoons minced fresh thyme
  4 teaspoons capers, drained
  2 garlic cloves, minced
  ¼ teaspoon salt
  ¼ teaspoon freshly ground black pepper

1. Preheat oven to 400°.

2. Cut 4 (14 x 12–inch) rectangles of foil. Place 1 fillet on each sheet.

3. Sprinkle each fillet evenly with lemon juice and next 5 ingredients. Fold foil in half over each fillet to form a packet; crimp edges to seal tightly. Place foil packets on a jelly-roll pan.

4. Bake at 400° for 15 minutes. Transfer fish to plates. Serve immediately. Yield: 4 servings (serving size: 1 fillet and 1½ tablespoons sauce).

Per serving: CALORIES 140 (10% from fat); FAT 1.5g (saturated fat 0g); PROTEIN 28.1g; CARBOHYDRATES 1.5g; FIBER 0.3g; CHOLESTEROL 102mg; IRON 2mg; SODIUM 353mg; CALCIUM 22mg

Sautéed Corn and Tomatoes ✔

prep: 3 minutes • **cook:** 4 minutes   **POINTS value: 1**

Heat a large nonstick skillet over medium-high heat. Coat pan with cooking spray. Add 1½ cups frozen whole-kernel corn, thawed; sauté 2 minutes or until tender. Add 1 (1-pound) container grape tomatoes, halved; sauté 1 minute. Add 1 tablespoon sliced fresh basil, ¼ teaspoon freshly ground black pepper, and ⅛ teaspoon salt; sauté 1 minute or until basil wilts. Yield: 4 servings (serving size: ¾ cup).

Per serving: CALORIES 85 (10% from fat); FAT 0.9g (saturated fat 0.1g); PROTEIN 3g; CARBOHYDRATES 19.8g; FIBER 3g; CHOLESTEROL 0mg; IRON 1mg; SODIUM 86mg; CALCIUM 10mg

Salmon with Sautéed Fennel

prep: 6 minutes • **cook:** 20 minutes   ***POINTS*** value: 7

Fennel, a member of the parsley family, has a bulbous base with celerylike stalks and feathery leaves. The stalks and bulb can be eaten like a vegetable, while the leaves are more like an herb. Fennel gets sweeter and its slight licorice flavor mellows when cooked, making fennel a delicious partner for the rich salmon.

  1 large fennel bulb
  4 (6-ounce) skinless salmon fillets (about 1 inch thick)
  ½ teaspoon salt, divided
  ⅛ teaspoon freshly ground black pepper
     Cooking spray
  1 cup julienne-cut yellow or orange bell pepper
  2 garlic cloves, thinly sliced
  ¾ cup dry white wine

1. Trim fennel bulb, and cut vertically into thin slices. Chop fronds to measure 2 tablespoons, discarding remaining fronds; set sliced fennel and chopped fronds aside.
2. Heat a large nonstick skillet over medium-high heat. Sprinkle fish with ¼ teaspoon salt and ⅛ teaspoon pepper; coat with cooking spray. Add fish to pan, and cook 2 minutes on each side or until brown; remove from pan.
3. Add fennel to pan; reduce heat to medium, and sauté 6 minutes or until crisp-tender. Stir in bell pepper and garlic, and cook 2 minutes. Add wine and remaining ¼ teaspoon salt; cook 2 minutes. Return fish to pan; cover and cook 6 minutes or until fish flakes easily when tested with a fork.
4. Divide fish and vegetable mixture among 4 plates. Sprinkle evenly with reserved chopped fronds. Yield: 4 servings (serving size: 1 fillet and about ⅔ cup vegetables).

Per serving: CALORIES 314 (39% from fat); FAT 13.3g (saturated fat 3.1g); PROTEIN 37.8g; CARBOHYDRATES 9.8g; FIBER 3.1g; CHOLESTEROL 87mg; IRON 1.6mg; SODIUM 419mg; CALCIUM 73mg

Lemon-Thyme Green Beans

prep: 2 minutes • **cook:** 4 minutes   ***POINTS*** value: 1

Pierce bag of 1 (12-ounce) package pretrimmed green beans with a fork. Microwave at HIGH 4 minutes or until tender. While beans cook, soften 2 tablespoons light stick butter. Combine butter with 1 teaspoon chopped fresh thyme and ½ teaspoon grated lemon rind in a large bowl. Add green beans; toss to coat. Yield: 4 servings (serving size: ¾ cup).

Per serving: CALORIES 62 (55% from fat); FAT 3.8g (saturated fat 2.3g); PROTEIN 1.8g; CARBOHYDRATES 6.7g; FIBER 2.7g; CHOLESTEROL 7mg; IRON 0.7mg; SODIUM 229mg; CALCIUM 41mg

Menu

POINTS value: 8

Salmon with Sautéed Fennel

Lemon-Thyme Green Beans

Grocery List

1 large fennel bulb

1 whole garlic head

1 medium yellow or orange bell pepper

1 (12-ounce) package pretrimmed green beans

1 small bunch fresh thyme

1 small lemon

1 (750-milliliter) bottle dry white wine

4 (6-ounce) skinless salmon fillets (about 1 inch thick)

Check staples: light stick butter, cooking spray, salt, and black pepper

Grocery List

1 small lemon

1 small bunch fresh parsley

1 whole garlic head

2 large zucchini

2 large yellow squash

1 (8-ounce) bottle fat-free balsamic vinaigrette

4 (6-ounce) salmon fillets

Check staples: light mayonnaise, stone-ground mustard, cooking spray, salt, and black pepper

Grilled Salmon with Mustard Sauce

prep: 6 minutes • **cook:** 8 minutes   *POINTS* value: 7

To cook this meal in 10 minutes, place the salmon, zucchini, and yellow squash on the grill at the same time. Fresh lemon juice and lemon rind balance the pungent flavor of the garlic in the creamy mustard sauce. Be sure to grate the rind before juicing the lemon.

  1 small lemon
  2 tablespoons light mayonnaise
  1 tablespoon stone-ground mustard
  1 tablespoon finely chopped parsley
  1   small garlic clove, minced
  ¼ teaspoon freshly ground black pepper, divided
  4 (6-ounce) salmon fillets
  ¼ teaspoon salt
  Cooking spray

1. Prepare grill.
2. Grate ¼ teaspoon rind from lemon. Squeeze lemon to measure 1½ teaspoons juice; reserve remaining lemon for another use. Combine lemon juice, rind, and next 4 ingredients in a small bowl, stirring with a whisk. Add ⅛ teaspoon black pepper, stirring well. Set aside.
3. Sprinkle fish with salt and remaining ⅛ teaspoon pepper. Place fish on grill rack coated with cooking spray. Cover and grill 4 to 5 minutes on each side or until fish flakes easily when tested with a fork. Transfer fish to a serving platter. Serve with mustard sauce. Yield: 4 servings (serving size: 1 fillet and 2½ teaspoons sauce).

Per serving: CALORIES 307 (46% from fat); FAT 15.6g (saturated fat 3.5g); PROTEIN 36.5g; CARBOHYDRATES 2g; FIBER 0.6g; CHOLESTEROL 89mg; IRON 0.7mg; SODIUM 345mg; CALCIUM 28mg

Balsamic Grilled Zucchini and Yellow Squash ☑.

prep: 3 minutes • **cook:** 10 minutes   *POINTS* value: 1

Prepare grill. Cut 2 large zucchini and 2 large yellow squash in half lengthwise. Brush cut sides of squash with ⅓ cup fat-free balsamic vinaigrette. Place squash on grill rack coated with cooking spray. Grill 5 minutes on each side or until squash are tender, basting with any remaining balsamic vinaigrette. Remove squash from grill, and cut into slices. Yield: 4 servings (serving size: 1 cup).

Per serving: CALORIES 67 (1% from fat); FAT 0.6g (saturated fat 0.1g); PROTEIN 3.9g; CARBOHYDRATES 14.6g; FIBER 3.6g; CHOLESTEROL 0mg; IRON 1.1mg; SODIUM 269mg; CALCIUM 48mg

pictured on page 119

Teriyaki Salmon with Mushrooms

prep: 3 minutes • **cook:** 15 minutes   *POINTS* value: 8

Get a healthy dose of omega-3 fatty acids, the fatty acids that lessen the risk of heart disease, from this pan-seared salmon served with a rich mushroom sauce. Substitute chicken broth for the sherry, if you prefer.

¼ cup dry sherry
¼ cup low-sodium teriyaki sauce
2 tablespoons light brown sugar
1 teaspoon canola oil
1 (8-ounce) package presliced baby portobello mushrooms
4 (6-ounce) skinless salmon fillets (about 1 to 1½ inches thick)

1. Combine first 3 ingredients in a small bowl; stir to dissolve sugar.
2. Heat oil in a large nonstick skillet over medium-high heat; add mushrooms, and sauté 4 minutes or until tender. Add ⅓ cup sherry mixture to mushrooms. Reduce heat, and simmer 1 to 2 minutes or until liquid almost evaporates. Spoon mushroom mixture into a bowl; set aside.
3. Heat pan over medium-high heat; add fish. Cook 3 to 4 minutes on each side or until browned on all sides. Add mushrooms and remaining sherry mixture to pan; cook 2 minutes. Transfer fish to a serving platter, and top with sauce and mushrooms. Yield: 4 servings (serving size: 1 fillet and 2 tablespoons mushroom mixture).

Per serving: CALORIES 335 (39% from fat); FAT 14.3g (saturated fat 3.2g); PROTEIN 37.6g; CARBOHYDRATES 9.5g; FIBER 0.9g; CHOLESTEROL 87mg; IRON 1.2mg; SODIUM 346mg; CALCIUM 32mg

Orange-Ginger Sugar Snaps

prep: 4 minutes • **cook:** 5 minutes   *POINTS* value: 1

Heat 1 teaspoon dark sesame oil in a nonstick skillet over medium heat; add 2 sliced green onions and ½ teaspoon grated peeled fresh ginger. Sauté 2 minutes; add 1 (8-ounce) package sugar snap peas, and sauté 2 minutes or just until crisp-tender. Remove from heat; stir in 1 teaspoon grated orange rind and ¼ teaspoon salt. Yield: 4 servings (serving size: ½ cup).

Per serving: CALORIES 40 (27% from fat); FAT 1.2g (saturated fat 0.2g); PROTEIN 1.5g; CARBOHYDRATES 5.4g; FIBER 1.6g; CHOLESTEROL 0mg; IRON 0.8mg; SODIUM 153mg; CALCIUM 46mg

Menu

POINTS value: 11

Teriyaki Salmon with Mushrooms

Orange-Ginger Sugar Snaps

½ cup whole-grain brown rice
POINTS value: 2

Grocery List

1 (8-ounce) package presliced baby portobello mushrooms

1 small bunch green onions

1 small piece ginger

1 (8-ounce) package sugar snap peas

1 small orange

1 (10-ounce) bottle low-sodium teriyaki sauce

1 (5-ounce) bottle dark sesame oil

1 (8.8-ounce) package precooked whole-grain brown rice (such as Uncle Ben's)

1 (750-milliliter) bottle dry sherry

4 (6-ounce) skinless salmon fillets (about 1 to 1½ inches thick)

Check staples: canola oil, light brown sugar, and salt

Grocery List

1 small lemon

1 small bunch fresh parsley

1 pound asparagus spears

1 (24-ounce) loaf light whole
wheat bread

1 (16-ounce) package uncooked
angel hair pasta

1 (3.5-ounce) jar capers

4 (6-ounce) snapper fillets
(about ¾ inch thick)

1 (750-milliliter) bottle dry
white wine

Check staples: light stick butter,
olive oil, salt, and black pepper

Snapper Piccata

prep: 5 minutes • **cook:** 9 minutes   *POINTS* value: 5

The wine and lemon juice are used to deglaze the skillet, capturing the browned bits of flavor that remain after the fish is cooked. You can substitute fat-free, less-sodium chicken broth for the wine, if desired. Cook the pasta and steam the asparagus while you prepare the fish so each dish will be ready at the same time.

1	tablespoon olive oil
4	(6-ounce) snapper fillets (about ¾ inch thick)
¼	teaspoon salt
¼	teaspoon freshly ground black pepper
½	cup dry white wine
2	tablespoons fresh lemon juice
2	tablespoons capers
2	tablespoons chopped fresh parsley

1. Heat oil in a large nonstick skillet over medium-high heat. Sprinkle fish evenly with salt and pepper. Add fish to pan, and cook 3 to 4 minutes on each side or until fish flakes easily when tested with a fork. Remove fish from pan; keep warm.

2. Add wine and juice to pan; bring to a boil. Reduce heat, and simmer 2 minutes or until slightly thick, scraping pan to loosen browned bits. Stir in capers and parsley. Spoon sauce evenly over fish. Yield: 4 servings (serving size: 1 fillet and about 1½ tablespoons sauce).

Per serving: CALORIES 205 (25% from fat); FAT 5.8g (saturated fat 1g); PROTEIN 35.4g; CARBOHYDRATES 1.4g; FIBER 0.1g; CHOLESTEROL 63mg; IRON 0.6mg; SODIUM 416mg; CALCIUM 63mg

Parsley-Buttered Pasta

prep: 3 minutes • **cook:** 10 minutes   *POINTS* value: 2

Cook 4 ounces angel hair pasta according to package directions, omitting salt and fat. While pasta cooks, place 1 (0.8-ounce) slice light whole wheat bread in a food processor; pulse 10 times or until coarse crumbs measure ½ cup. Combine cooked pasta, breadcrumbs, 1 tablespoon light stick butter, 2 teaspoons chopped fresh parsley, ¼ teaspoon salt, and ⅛ teaspoon freshly ground black pepper; toss gently. Serve immediately. Yield: 4 servings (serving size: ½ cup).

Per serving: CALORIES 125 (17% from fat); FAT 2.3g (saturated fat 1g); PROTEIN 4.4g; CARBOHYDRATES 23.3g; FIBER 1.6g; CHOLESTEROL 4mg; IRON 1.2mg; SODIUM 196mg; CALCIUM 17mg

Italian Fish in Foil ☑

prep: 11 minutes • **cook:** 17 minutes • **other:** 2 minutes   *POINTS* value: 4

Flavorful liquid will escape from the vegetables and fish during cooking. Spoon this liquid over the fish before serving, and use the ciabatta to soak up the juices.

- 2 cups sliced zucchini (about 2 large)
- 4 (6-ounce) red snapper or other firm white fish fillets
- ½ teaspoon salt
- ½ teaspoon freshly ground black pepper
- ¾ cup thinly sliced onion
- 1 cup halved grape tomatoes
- ⅓ cup torn basil leaves

1. Preheat oven to 450°.
2. Cut 4 (20 x 12–inch) rectangles of foil.
3. Place ½ cup zucchini on each sheet. Place fillets on top of zucchini; sprinkle evenly with salt and pepper. Layer onion, tomatoes, and basil evenly over fillets. Fold foil in half over each fillet to form a packet; crimp edges to seal tightly. Place foil packets on a baking sheet.
4. Bake at 450° for 17 minutes. Remove from oven, and let stand 2 minutes. Serve immediately. Yield: 4 servings (serving size: 1 fillet and about ¾ cup vegetables).

Per serving: CALORIES 197 (12% from fat); FAT 2.5g (saturated fat 0.5g); PROTEIN 36.3g; CARBOHYDRATES 5.9g; FIBER 1.7g; CHOLESTEROL 63mg; IRON 0.8mg; SODIUM 409mg; CALCIUM 79mg

Sautéed Kale with Roasted Red Bell Peppers

prep: 1 minute • **cook:** 13 minutes   *POINTS* value: 1

Heat a large nonstick skillet over medium-high heat. Coat pan with olive oil–flavored cooking spray. Add 6 cups prechopped kale; sauté 3 minutes. Add 2 garlic cloves, minced, and cook 2 minutes. Add ¼ cup water; cover and cook 6 to 8 minutes or until kale is tender. Add ½ cup sliced bottled roasted red bell peppers, 1 tablespoon balsamic vinegar, ½ teaspoon sugar, and ¼ teaspoon salt. Cook, uncovered, over medium-high heat until liquid evaporates. Yield: 4 servings (serving size: ¾ cup).

Per serving: CALORIES 63 (9% from fat); FAT 0.7g (saturated fat 0.1g); PROTEIN 3.4g; CARBOHYDRATES 12.7g; FIBER 2g; CHOLESTEROL 0mg; IRON 1.8mg; SODIUM 267mg; CALCIUM 140mg

Menu

POINTS value: 7

Italian Fish in Foil

Sautéed Kale with Roasted Red Bell Peppers

1 (1-ounce) slice ciabatta
POINTS value: 2

Grocery List

2 large zucchini

1 small onion

1 (1-pound) container grape tomatoes

1 small bunch fresh basil

1 (16-ounce) package prechopped kale

1 whole garlic head

1 (14-ounce) loaf ciabatta (such as Archer Farms)

1 (12-ounce) bottle roasted red bell peppers

4 (6-ounce) red snapper or other firm white fish fillets

Check staples: olive oil–flavored cooking spray, balsamic vinegar, sugar, salt, and black pepper

Snapper with Red Pepper and Fennel

½ cup mashed sweet potatoes
POINTS value: 1

Grocery List

1 large fennel bulb

1 (12-ounce) bottle roasted red bell peppers

1 (7-ounce) jar pitted kalamata olives

1 (24-ounce) container refrigerated mashed sweet potatoes

4 (6-ounce) red snapper fillets

Check staples: olive oil–flavored cooking spray, red wine vinegar, salt, and black pepper

Snapper with Red Pepper and Fennel ☑.

prep: 8 minutes • **cook:** 15 minutes   *POINTS* value: 5

Chop the bell peppers and olives and microwave the mashed sweet potatoes while the fish bakes.

 4 (6-ounce) red snapper fillets
Olive oil–flavored cooking spray
¼ teaspoon salt
¼ teaspoon freshly ground black pepper
 1 large fennel bulb, thinly sliced
¾ cup chopped bottled roasted red bell peppers
⅓ cup chopped pitted kalamata olives
 2 teaspoons red wine vinegar

1. Preheat oven to 450°.
2. Place fish in a 13 x 9–inch baking dish coated with cooking spray. Sprinkle evenly with ¼ teaspoon salt and ¼ teaspoon black pepper.
3. Arrange fennel on top of and around fish. Bake at 450° for 15 minutes or until fish flakes easily when tested with a fork. Carefully remove fish from baking dish, and place on a serving plate; keep warm. Add bell pepper, olives, and vinegar to fennel in baking dish; toss well to coat. Spoon sauce evenly over fish. Yield: 4 servings (serving size: 1 fillet and about ½ cup sauce).

Per serving: CALORIES 228 (22% from fat); FAT 5.5g (saturated fat 0.9g); PROTEIN 35.8g; CARBOHYDRATES 6.7g; FIBER 1.9g; CHOLESTEROL 63mg; IRON 0.8mg; SODIUM 743mg; CALCIUM 86mg

Hoisin Tuna Skewers

prep: 7 minutes • **cook:** 4 minutes • **other:** 10 minutes   *POINTS* value: 5

We've threaded the tuna pieces on separate skewers from the bell pepper and pineapple to ensure even cooking and caramelization. If using wooden skewers, allow 30 minutes for them to soak in water so they won't burn on the grill.

   3   tablespoons hoisin sauce
1½   tablespoons water
   4   garlic cloves, minced
1½   cups fresh pineapple, cut into 1-inch pieces
   1   large red bell pepper, cut into 1-inch pieces
1½   pounds tuna steaks, trimmed and cut into 1-inch pieces
      Cooking spray

1. Combine first 3 ingredients in a small bowl; set aside.
2. Thread pineapple and bell pepper pieces alternately onto 4 (8-inch) skewers. Thread tuna pieces evenly onto 4 (8-inch) skewers. Brush threaded skewers evenly with hoisin mixture. Set aside to marinate for 10 minutes.
3. Prepare grill.
4. Place skewers on grill rack coated with cooking spray. Cover and grill 2 to 3 minutes on each side until fish is medium-rare or desired degree of doneness, and pineapple and bell pepper pieces begin to brown around the edges. Yield: 4 servings (serving size: 1 tuna skewer and 1 pineapple-pepper skewer).

Per serving: CALORIES 249 (8% from fat); FAT 2.2g (saturated fat 0.5g); PROTEIN 41g; CARBOHYDRATES 15.1g; FIBER 1.1g; CHOLESTEROL 77mg; IRON 1.7mg; SODIUM 259mg; CALCIUM 48mg

Asian Coleslaw

prep: 4 minutes   *POINTS* value: 1

Place 1 cup frozen shelled edamame in a colander, and rinse under cool running water to thaw; drain well. Combine edamame, 4 cups angel hair slaw, ¼ cup light sesame ginger dressing (such as Newman's Own), and 2 tablespoons chopped fresh cilantro in a large bowl. Toss well. Yield: 4 servings (serving size: ¾ cup).

Per serving: CALORIES 82 (31% from fat); FAT 2.8g (saturated fat 0.2g); PROTEIN 4.9g; CARBOHYDRATES 9.7g; FIBER 3.4g; CHOLESTEROL 0mg; IRON 0.9mg; SODIUM 211mg; CALCIUM 25mg

Menu

POINTS value: 6

Hoisin Tuna Skewers

Asian Coleslaw

Grocery List

1 whole garlic head

1 large red bell pepper

1 cored fresh pineapple

1 (10-ounce) package angel hair slaw

1 small bunch fresh cilantro

1 (7.5-ounce) jar hoisin sauce

1 (16-ounce) bottle light sesame ginger dressing (such as Newman's Own)

1 (12-ounce) package frozen shelled edamame

1½ pounds tuna steaks

Check staples: cooking spray

pictured on page 43

Scallops with Lemon-Basil Sauce

prep: 3 minutes • **cook:** 12 minutes

POINTS value: 4

For speed and convenience, prepare the entire package of pasta. Plan to serve 2 cups when you prepare it, and use the rest for tomorrow's lunch or dinner.

Menu

POINTS value: 8

Scallops with Lemon-Basil Sauce

Spinach Fettuccine

1 cup sliced strawberries
POINTS **value: 1**

Grocery List

1 large lemon

1 small bunch fresh basil

1 (16-ounce) container strawberries

1 (9-ounce) package spinach fettuccine

1 (750-milliliter) bottle dry white wine

1 (8-ounce) wedge Parmesan cheese

1½ pounds sea scallops

Check staples: butter, cornstarch, salt, and black pepper

1	large lemon
1½	pounds sea scallops
¼	teaspoon salt, divided
¼	teaspoon freshly ground black pepper, divided
1	tablespoon butter, divided
¾	cup dry white wine
1	tablespoon water
½	teaspoon cornstarch
1	tablespoon finely chopped fresh basil

1. Finely grate lemon rind, reserving ¼ teaspoon. Squeeze lemon, reserving 2 tablespoons juice. Pat scallops dry with paper towels.

2. Sprinkle scallops with ⅛ teaspoon each salt and pepper. Melt 2 teaspoons butter in a large nonstick skillet over medium heat. Add scallops; cook 3 to 4 minutes on each side or until done. Remove scallops from pan; keep warm.

3. Add wine and reserved lemon juice to pan, and bring to a boil. Reduce heat, and simmer 2 minutes, stirring to loosen browned bits from bottom of pan. Combine water and cornstarch; add to pan. Cook, stirring constantly, 2 minutes or until sauce begins to thicken. Add reserved lemon rind, remaining 1 teaspoon butter, remaining ⅛ teaspoon each salt and pepper, and basil. Remove from heat. Serve over scallops. Yield: 4 servings (serving size: 3 scallops and about 1 tablespoon sauce).

Per serving: CALORIES 185 (20% from fat); FAT 4.1g (saturated fat 1.9g); PROTEIN 28.9g; CARBOHYDRATES 7g; FIBER 0.7g; CHOLESTEROL 64mg; IRON 0.8mg; SODIUM 447mg; CALCIUM 51mg

Spinach Fettuccine

prep: 1 minute • **cook:** 6 minutes

POINTS value: 3

Cook 1 (9-ounce) package fresh spinach fettuccine according to package directions, omitting salt and fat. Drain. Combine cooked pasta, ⅓ cup grated fresh Parmesan cheese, and 2 tablespoons butter; toss well. Yield: 7 servings (serving size: about ½ cup).

Per serving: CALORIES 157 (32% from fat); FAT 5.5g (saturated fat 3g); PROTEIN 6.4g; CARBOHYDRATES 20.3g; FIBER 1.2g; CHOLESTEROL 39mg; IRON 1.2mg; SODIUM 128mg; CALCIUM 93mg

Seared Scallops with Spicy Pepper Sauce

prep: 5 minutes • **cook:** 5 minutes   *POINTS* value: 5

The key to getting a beautiful brown sear is to pat the scallops dry before cooking, sear them in a hot skillet, and, while they cook, move them only to turn them over. The subtle hint of heat from the crushed red pepper complements the sweetness from the bottled roasted red bell peppers in the intensely flavored sauce.

 2 garlic cloves
 ½ cup bottled roasted red bell peppers, drained
 ¼ cup light mayonnaise
 ½ teaspoon salt, divided
 ⅛ teaspoon crushed red pepper
1½ pounds sea scallops
 ¼ teaspoon freshly ground black pepper
 2 teaspoons olive oil

1. Process garlic in a food processor until finely minced. Add roasted red bell peppers, mayonnaise, ¼ teaspoon salt, and crushed red pepper; process until well combined.
2. Pat scallops dry with paper towels. Sprinkle with remaining ¼ teaspoon salt and black pepper. Heat oil in a large nonstick skillet over medium-high heat until hot. Add scallops to pan, and cook 2 to 3 minutes on each side or until browned. Spoon sauce onto plates; top with scallops. Serve immediately. Yield: 4 servings (serving size: about 3 scallops and 2 tablespoons sauce).

Per serving: CALORIES 228 (34% from fat); FAT 8.7g (saturated fat 1.5g); PROTEIN 28.7g; CARBOHYDRATES 6.6g; FIBER 0.1g; CHOLESTEROL 61mg; IRON 0.6mg; SODIUM 767mg; CALCIUM 45mg

Mushroom–Brown Rice Pilaf

prep: 1 minute • **cook:** 4 minutes   *POINTS* value: 2

Heat 1 teaspoon olive oil in a nonstick skillet over medium-high heat; add 1 cup presliced baby portobello mushrooms, and cook 2 minutes. Add ½ cup halved grape tomatoes and 1 minced garlic clove; cook 1 minute or until mushrooms are tender. While mushrooms cook, heat 2 (4.4-ounce) containers precooked whole-grain brown rice (such as Success) in the microwave according to package directions. Stir together mushrooms, rice, ¼ teaspoon salt, and ⅛ teaspoon freshly ground black pepper. Yield: 4 servings (serving size: about ½ cup).

Per serving: CALORIES 108 (30% from fat); FAT 3.6g (saturated fat 0.4g); PROTEIN 2.2g; CARBOHYDRATES 15.9g; FIBER 1.4g; CHOLESTEROL 0mg; IRON 0.3mg; SODIUM 150mg; CALCIUM 16mg

Menu

POINTS value: 7

Seared Scallops with Spicy Pepper Sauce

Mushroom–Brown Rice Pilaf

1 cup baby spinach salad with fat-free red wine vinaigrette ☑.
POINTS value: 0

Grocery List

1 whole garlic head

1 (8-ounce) package presliced baby portobello mushrooms

1 (1-pound) package grape tomatoes

1 (5- or 6-ounce) package fresh baby spinach

1 (12-ounce) bottle roasted red bell peppers

1 (8-ounce) bottle fat-free red wine vinaigrette

1 (8.8-ounce) package precooked whole-grain brown rice (such as Success)

1½ pounds sea scallops

Check staples: olive oil, light mayonnaise, crushed red pepper, salt, and black pepper

Menu

POINTS value: 6

Barbecue Shrimp Pizza

Grilled Corn on the Cob with Chive Butter

Grocery List

1 (8-ounce) container presliced red onion

1 small bunch fresh cilantro

1 small bunch fresh chives

8 ears shucked corn

1 (18-ounce) bottle barbecue sauce

1 (10-ounce) Italian cheese-flavored thin pizza crust (such as Boboli)

1 (4-ounce) package shredded part-skim mozzarella cheese

½ pound cooked peeled shrimp

Check staples: light stick butter and cooking spray

Barbecue Shrimp Pizza

prep: 3 minutes • **cook:** 12 minutes   *POINTS* value: 4

We've replaced traditional pizza sauce with a store-bought barbecue sauce for this quick-to-prepare pizza. Bake the crust directly on the rack to give it a crisp texture and a golden color.

¼   cup barbecue sauce
1   (10-ounce) Italian cheese-flavored thin pizza crust (such as Boboli)
½   pound cooked peeled shrimp, coarsely chopped
⅓   cup presliced red onion
¾   cup (3 ounces) shredded part-skim mozzarella cheese
2   tablespoons chopped fresh cilantro

1. Preheat oven to 450°.

2. Spread barbecue sauce over pizza crust. Arrange shrimp and onion over sauce; sprinkle evenly with cheese. Place pizza crust directly on oven rack. Bake at 450° for 12 minutes or until lightly browned and bubbly. Sprinkle fresh cilantro evenly over pizza. Cut into 8 slices. Yield: 8 servings (serving size: 1 slice).

Per serving: CALORIES 184 (23% from fat); FAT 4.6g (saturated fat 2.4g); PROTEIN 12.5g; CARBOHYDRATES 22.2g; FIBER 0.7g; CHOLESTEROL 61mg; IRON 2mg; SODIUM 385mg; CALCIUM 140mg

Grilled Corn on the Cob with Chive Butter

prep: 3 minutes • **cook:** 12 minutes   *POINTS* value: 2

Prepare grill. Coat 8 ears shucked corn with cooking spray. Place corn on grill rack; cover and grill 6 minutes on each side or until slightly charred. While corn grills, combine ¼ cup softened light stick butter and 2 tablespoons chopped fresh chives. Brush butter mixture over grilled corn. Yield: 8 servings (serving size: 1 ear of corn).

Per serving: CALORIES 103 (31% from fat); FAT 3.6g (saturated fat 1.2g); PROTEIN 2.9g; CARBOHYDRATES 17.2g; FIBER 2.5g; CHOLESTEROL 3mg; IRON 0.5mg; SODIUM 61mg; CALCIUM 2mg

Honey Mustard Shrimp and Peach Kebabs

prep: 20 minutes • **cook:** 6 minutes   *POINTS* value: 6

The light honey mustard dressing becomes a quick glaze for the kebabs and potatoes. Place the potatoes on the grill before the shrimp to ensure they are done at the same time.

  3   tablespoons light honey mustard dressing (such as Ken's)
  2   tablespoons light stick butter, melted
1½ pounds peeled and deveined large shrimp
  2   large peaches, peeled, pitted, and each cut into 6 wedges
  4   green onions, cut into 2-inch lengths
Cooking spray

1. Prepare grill.
2. Combine honey mustard dressing and butter in a small bowl. Thread shrimp, peach wedges, and green onions evenly onto 6 (12-inch) skewers; brush evenly with honey mustard mixture.
3. Place skewers on grill rack coated with cooking spray. Grill, covered, 3 minutes on each side or until shrimp turn pink. Yield: 3 servings (serving size: 2 kebabs).

Per serving: CALORIES 299 (26% from fat); FAT 8.7g (saturated fat 3.1g); PROTEIN 41.5g; CARBOHYDRATES 17.9g; FIBER 2.3g; CHOLESTEROL 349mg; IRON 6mg; SODIUM 549mg; CALCIUM 95mg

Grilled Sweet Potatoes

prep: 2 minutes • **cook:** 13 minutes   *POINTS* value: 1

Prepare grill. Cut 3 small peeled sweet potatoes lengthwise into 4 slices. Arrange potato slices in a single layer on a large microwave-safe dish. Microwave at HIGH 5 minutes or just until tender. While potato cooks, combine 1 tablespoon light honey mustard dressing (such as Ken's) and ½ tablespoon melted light stick butter in a small bowl. Brush potatoes evenly with half of honey mustard mixture. Place potato slices on grill rack coated with cooking spray. Grill potato slices 8 to 10 minutes, turning after 4 minutes to brush potato slices with remaining honey mustard mixture. Yield: 3 servings (serving size: about 4 potato slices).

Per serving: CALORIES 77 (22% from fat); FAT 1.9g (saturated fat 0.7g); PROTEIN 2.5g; CARBOHYDRATES 14.3g; FIBER 2g; CHOLESTEROL 3mg; IRON 0.4mg; SODIUM 69mg; CALCIUM 23mg

---

Menu

POINTS value: 7

Honey Mustard Shrimp and Peach Kebabs

Grilled Sweet Potatoes

Grocery List

2 large peaches

1 small bunch green onions

3 small sweet potatoes

1 (8-ounce) bottle light honey mustard dressing (such as Ken's)

1½ pounds peeled and deveined large shrimp

Check staples: light stick butter and cooking spray

Grocery List

1 medium onion

1 large lemon

1 small bunch fresh parsley

1 (9-ounce) box raisins

1 (14.5-ounce) can petite diced tomatoes

1 (1.7-ounce) jar garam masala

1 (10-ounce) box uncooked plain couscous

1½ pounds peeled and deveined large shrimp

Check staples: cooking spray, salt, and black pepper

Moroccan Shrimp

prep: 5 minutes • **cook:** 9 minutes   *POINTS* value: 4

Look for garam masala, a peppery Indian spice blend, in the spice aisle at your supermarket.

   Cooking spray
  1 cup chopped onion
  1 teaspoon garam masala
1½ pounds peeled and deveined large shrimp
  1 (14.5-ounce) can petite diced tomatoes
½ cup raisins
½ teaspoon salt
½ teaspoon freshly ground black pepper

1. Heat a large nonstick skillet over medium-high heat. Coat pan with cooking spray. Add onion; cook 3 minutes or until tender. Add garam masala; cook 1 minute, stirring constantly. Add shrimp; cook 3 minutes or until shrimp are done, stirring occasionally.
2. Add tomatoes, raisins, salt, and pepper; cook 2 minutes or until thoroughly heated. Serve immediately. Yield: 4 servings (serving size: 1 cup).

Per serving: CALORIES 227 (6% from fat); FAT 1.5g (saturated fat 0.4g); PROTEIN 29g; CARBOHYDRATES 25.1g; FIBER 3.1g; CHOLESTEROL 252mg; IRON 4.8mg; SODIUM 715mg; CALCIUM 87mg

Lemon-Parsley Couscous

prep: 2 minutes • **cook:** 4 minutes • **other:** 5 minutes   *POINTS* value: 2

Prepare ¾ cup uncooked plain couscous according to package directions, omitting salt and fat. Grate ½ teaspoon rind from 1 lemon. Squeeze lemon to measure 2 tablespoons juice; reserve remaining lemon for another use. Combine couscous with lemon rind, lemon juice, and 2 teaspoons fresh chopped parsley. Yield: 4 servings (serving size: about ½ cup).

Per serving: CALORIES 124 (2% from fat); FAT 0.2g (saturated fat 0g); PROTEIN 4.2g; CARBOHYDRATES 25.9g; FIBER 1.7g; CHOLESTEROL 0mg; IRON 0.4mg; SODIUM 4mg; CALCIUM 10mg

Meatless Main Dishes

Salsa-Vegetable Stuffed Peppers

½ cup brown rice

POINTS value: 2

Grocery List

4 medium green bell peppers

1 medium zucchini

1 (24-ounce) bottle salsa

1 (15-ounce) can black beans

1 (8.8-ounce) package precooked whole-grain brown rice (such as Uncle Ben's)

1 (8-ounce) package reduced-fat shredded Cheddar cheese

Salsa-Vegetable Stuffed Peppers

prep: 12 minutes • **cook:** 4 hours   *POINTS* value: 3

Serve these versatile stuffed peppers with brown rice for a meatless meal or as a hearty side dish to accompany grilled pork chops. You control the spiciness with the type of salsa you use. Serve with 2 tablespoons reduced-fat sour cream for an additional *POINTS* value of 1.

    4 medium green bell peppers
    2 cups bottled salsa, divided
    2 cups chopped zucchini (about 1 medium)
    1 (15-ounce) can black beans, rinsed and drained
    ½ cup (2 ounces) reduced-fat shredded Cheddar cheese

1. Cut tops off bell peppers; discard tops, seeds, and membranes.
2. Combine 1 cup salsa, zucchini, and beans in a medium bowl; stir well. Divide vegetable mixture evenly among peppers.
3. Spoon remaining 1 cup salsa into a 6-quart oval electric slow cooker. Place stuffed peppers upright in cooker; cover and cook on LOW 4 hours. Sprinkle peppers evenly with cheese. Yield: 4 servings (serving size: 1 stuffed pepper).

Per serving: CALORIES 148 (27% from fat); FAT 4.5g (saturated fat 2.3g); PROTEIN 9.9g; CARBOHYDRATES 25g; FIBER 7.8g; CHOLESTEROL 11mg; IRON 1.6mg; SODIUM 868mg; CALCIUM 175mg

pictured on page 125

Black Bean and Spinach Quesadillas

prep: 9 minutes • **cook:** 13 minutes   *POINTS* value: 5

You'll have about ½ cup of refried beans left over after making the quesadillas. Cover and refrigerate the leftover beans. Later in the week, combine them with ½ cup salsa and serve with raw veggies or baked tortilla chips. About ¼ cup of the dip will have a *POINTS* value of 1.

  2 cups refried black beans
½ cup refrigerated fresh salsa
Olive oil–flavored cooking spray
  1 (5- or 6-ounce) package fresh baby spinach, coarsely chopped
  6 (8½-inch) garden spinach and vegetable tortillas (such as Tumaro's)
¾ cup (3 ounces) preshredded reduced-fat 4-cheese Mexican blend cheese
Additional refrigerated fresh salsa (optional)

1. Combine black beans and ½ cup salsa; set aside.
2. Heat a large nonstick skillet over medium-high heat. Coat pan with cooking spray. Add spinach; sauté 1 minute or just until spinach wilts. Remove pan from heat; set aside.
3. Spread ¼ cup black bean mixture on half of each tortilla, leaving a ¼-inch margin. Top evenly with spinach and cheese. Fold each tortilla in half.
4. Wipe pan dry with a paper towel; heat pan over medium heat. Coat pan with cooking spray. Place 2 quesadillas in pan. Cook 2 to 3 minutes on each side or until lightly browned and cheese melts. Repeat with remaining quesadillas. Cut into wedges. Serve with additional salsa, if desired. Yield: 6 servings (serving size: 1 quesadilla).

Per serving: CALORIES 252 (23% from fat); FAT 6.3g (saturated fat 2g); PROTEIN 12.7g; CARBOHYDRATES 39.2g; FIBER 6.3g; CHOLESTEROL 10mg; IRON 4.8mg; SODIUM 527mg; CALCIUM 285mg

Menu

POINTS value: 7

Black Bean and Spinach Quesadillas

1 cup Mojito Slush (page 22)
POINTS value: 2

Grocery List

1 (16-ounce) container refrigerated fresh salsa

1 (5- or 6-ounce) package fresh baby spinach

9 medium limes

1 small bunch fresh mint

1 (12.7-ounce) package (8½-inch) garden spinach and vegetable tortillas (such as Tumaro's)

1 (20.5-ounce) can refried black beans

1 pint white rum

1 (8-ounce) package preshredded reduced-fat 4-cheese Mexican blend cheese

Check staples: olive oil–flavored cooking spray and "measures-like-sugar" calorie-free sweetener (such as Splenda)

Menu

POINTS value: 5

Italian-Style White Beans

Spicy Wilted Spinach ☑

Grocery List

1 whole garlic head

1 small bunch fresh sage

4 plum tomatoes

1 small lemon

1 (5- or 6-ounce) package fresh baby spinach

2 (15-ounce) cans cannellini beans

1 (8-ounce) wedge Parmesan cheese

Check staples: olive oil, crushed red pepper, salt, and black pepper

Italian-Style White Beans

prep: 6 minutes • **cook:** 5 minutes   *POINTS* value: 4

Keep a wedge of fresh Parmesan cheese in the refrigerator, and you can quickly add big flavor to many dishes. It's better to grate, shred, or shave only the amount of cheese that you need at one time. Keep the rest tightly wrapped in plastic in the refrigerator up to 6 months.

1½ tablespoons olive oil
 4 garlic cloves, minced
 2 tablespoons coarsely chopped fresh sage
 2 (15-ounce) cans cannellini beans, rinsed and drained
 2 cups diced plum tomato (about 4 tomatoes)
Freshly ground black pepper
¼ cup (1 ounce) shaved fresh Parmesan cheese

1. Heat oil in a large nonstick skillet over medium heat. Add garlic; sauté 1 minute or until tender. Add sage; cook 1 minute. Add beans to pan, stirring well. Cook over medium heat until thoroughly heated, stirring occasionally. Remove from heat.
2. Add tomato to pan, and toss gently; sprinkle with black pepper. Top with cheese. Yield: 4 servings (serving size: 1¼ cups).

Per serving: CALORIES 193 (36% from fat); FAT 7.8g (saturated fat 1.9g); PROTEIN 8.5g; CARBOHYDRATES 22.5g; FIBER 6g; CHOLESTEROL 5mg; IRON 2.1mg; SODIUM 397mg; CALCIUM 143mg

Spicy Wilted Spinach ☑

prep: 3 minutes • **cook:** 4 minutes   *POINTS* value: 1

Heat 1 tablespoon olive oil in a large nonstick skillet over medium-high heat. Add 1 minced garlic clove and ¼ teaspoon crushed red pepper; sauté 2 minutes. Add 1 (5- or 6-ounce) package fresh baby spinach, and cook 1 minute or just until spinach begins to wilt. Sprinkle spinach mixture with ⅛ teaspoon salt, and serve immediately with lemon wedges. Yield: 4 servings (serving size: 1¼ cups spinach and 1 lemon wedge).

Per serving: CALORIES 50 (56% from fat); FAT 3.5g (saturated fat 0.5g); PROTEIN 1.1g; CARBOHYDRATES 5.1g; FIBER 2.1g; CHOLESTEROL 0mg; IRON 1.4mg; SODIUM 140mg; CALCIUM 32mg

pictured on page 33

Goat Cheese and Asparagus Pizza

prep: 10 minutes • **cook:** 10 minutes   *POINTS* value: 7

For a crispier crust, lightly coat the crust with cooking spray before adding the toppings. While the pizza bakes, prepare the veggies for the salad.

⅓ cup commercial pesto
1 (14-ounce) Italian cheese-flavored pizza crust (such as Boboli)
2 plum tomatoes, thinly sliced
8 asparagus spears, cut into 1-inch pieces
¾ cup (3 ounces) crumbled goat cheese

1. Preheat oven to 450°.
2. Spread pesto over pizza crust, and top with tomato, asparagus, and cheese.
3. Place pizza on center rack in oven; bake at 450° for 10 to 12 minutes or until asparagus is crisp-tender and cheese melts. Yield: 6 servings (serving size: 1 slice).

Per serving: CALORIES 301 (42% from fat); FAT 14g (saturated fat 5.2g); PROTEIN 12.2g; CARBOHYDRATES 31.2g; FIBER 1.7g; CHOLESTEROL 16mg; IRON 2.8mg; SODIUM 543mg; CALCIUM 257mg

Watercress, Hearts of Palm, and Radicchio Salad

prep: 5 minutes   *POINTS* value: 1

Combine 1 (4-ounce) package watercress; 1 (14-ounce) can hearts of palm, drained and sliced; ½ cup thinly sliced radicchio; and ¼ cup light olive oil and vinegar dressing in a large bowl. Toss gently. Serve immediately. Yield: 6 servings (serving size: about 1 cup).

Per serving: CALORIES 37 (56% from fat); FAT 2.3g (saturated fat 0.2g); PROTEIN 1.8g; CARBOHYDRATES 3.7g; FIBER 1.3g; CHOLESTEROL 0mg; IRON 1.6mg; SODIUM 297mg; CALCIUM 56mg

Menu

POINTS value: 8

Goat Cheese and Asparagus Pizza

Watercress, Hearts of Palm, and Radicchio Salad

Grocery List

2 plum tomatoes

8 asparagus spears (about 8 ounces)

1 (4-ounce) package watercress

1 small head radicchio

1 (14-ounce) can hearts of palm

1 (16-ounce) bottle light olive oil and vinegar dressing

1 (10-ounce) jar commercial pesto

1 (14-ounce) Italian cheese-flavored pizza crust (such as Boboli)

1 (4-ounce) package crumbled goat cheese

pictured on page 116

Mini White Pizzas with Vegetables

Caesar Salad

Grocery List

1 medium zucchini

1 small red onion

1 (22-ounce) package romaine hearts

1 (12-ounce) package 6-inch whole wheat pitas

1 (14-ounce) bottle light Caesar dressing

1 (5-ounce) package large-cut Caesar-flavored croutons

1 (6.5-ounce) container light garlic-and-herbs spreadable cheese (such as Alouette Light)

1 (6-ounce) container shredded Asiago cheese

1 (8-ounce) wedge Parmesan cheese

Check staples: olive oil–flavored cooking spray, salt, and black pepper

Mini White Pizzas with Vegetables

prep: 5 minutes • **cook:** 9 minutes   *POINTS* value: 5

We used whole wheat pita rounds for portion control and to achieve a quicker bake time compared to a regular-sized pizza. For a Greek-inspired flavor variation, substitute hummus for the spreadable cheese. The *POINTS* value per serving will remain the same.

   4   (6-inch) whole wheat pitas
   Olive oil–flavored cooking spray
   1   medium zucchini, thinly sliced
   ¼   cup thinly sliced red onion, separated into rings
   ¼   teaspoon freshly ground black pepper
   ⅛   teaspoon salt
   ½   cup light garlic-and-herbs spreadable cheese (such as Alouette Light)
   6   tablespoons shredded Asiago cheese

1. Preheat broiler.

2. Place pitas on a baking sheet; broil 3 minutes.

3. Heat a nonstick skillet over medium-high heat. Coat pan with cooking spray. Add zucchini, onion, black pepper, and salt; sauté 3 minutes or until vegetables are crisp-tender.

4. Remove pitas from oven, and spread 2 tablespoons garlic-and-herbs spreadable cheese over each pita. Top evenly with vegetables and Asiago cheese. Broil 3 minutes or until edges are lightly browned and cheese melts. Yield: 4 servings (serving size: 1 pizza).

Per serving: CALORIES 272 (29% from fat); FAT 8.7g (saturated fat 4.6g); PROTEIN 11.9g; CARBOHYDRATES 40.2g; FIBER 5.5g; CHOLESTEROL 24mg; IRON 2.2mg; SODIUM 505mg; CALCIUM 137mg

Caesar Salad

prep: 8 minutes   *POINTS* value: 2

Cut 2 romaine hearts in half lengthwise. Top each romaine half with 1 tablespoon light Caesar dressing, 1 tablespoon freshly grated Parmesan cheese, and 2 halved large-cut Caesar-flavored croutons. Yield: 4 servings (serving size: 1 salad).

Per serving: CALORIES 102 (54% from fat); FAT 6.1g (saturated fat 1.5g); PROTEIN 5.1g; CARBOHYDRATES 7.8g; FIBER 1.2g; CHOLESTEROL 10mg; IRON 1.3mg; SODIUM 342mg; CALCIUM 149mg

Ravioli with Butternut Squash Sauce

prep: 1 minute • **cook:** 14 minutes

POINTS value: 6

The rich color and creamy texture of the butternut squash sauce is reminiscent of traditional pasta sauces chock-full of heavy cream. We prefer the nutty flavor that the dry sherry gives the sauce, but you can substitute 2 tablespoons of vegetable broth, if you'd like.

  1 (9-ounce) package refrigerated whole wheat 4-cheese ravioli
  1 (12-ounce) package frozen pureed butternut squash
  ¼ cup 1% low-fat milk
  1 tablespoon dry sherry
  ¼ teaspoon salt
  ¼ teaspoon freshly ground black pepper
  ¹⁄₁₆ teaspoon ground nutmeg
  3 tablespoons chopped walnuts, toasted

1. Cook ravioli according to package directions; drain and place in a serving bowl.
2. While ravioli cooks, prepare butternut squash according to microwave directions on package. Combine butternut squash with milk in a medium saucepan over medium heat. Add sherry and next 3 ingredients. Cook 5 minutes or until hot. Pour sauce over cooked ravioli; toss well to coat. Top with chopped walnuts. Yield: 4 servings (serving size: 1 cup).

Per serving: CALORIES 291 (39% from fat); FAT 12.6g (saturated fat 4.6g); PROTEIN 11.2g; CARBOHYDRATES 33.3g; FIBER 4.2g; CHOLESTEROL 43mg; IRON 1.8mg; SODIUM 777mg; CALCIUM 132mg

Pear, Strawberry, and Spinach Salad

prep: 5 minutes

POINTS value: 1

Core 1 pear, and cut lengthwise into ¼-inch-thick slices; halve 10 strawberries. Combine pear slices and strawberry halves with 1 (5- or 6-ounce) package fresh baby spinach and ¼ cup light balsamic vinaigrette; toss gently. Yield: 4 servings (serving size: 1¾ cups).

Per serving: CALORIES 72 (26% from fat); FAT 2.1g (saturated fat 0.3g); PROTEIN 1.4g; CARBOHYDRATES 13.6g; FIBER 3.9g; CHOLESTEROL 0mg; IRON 1.4mg; SODIUM 303mg; CALCIUM 38mg

Menu

POINTS value: 7

Ravioli with Butternut Squash Sauce

Pear, Strawberry, and Spinach Salad

Grocery List

1 ripe pear

1 (16-ounce) container strawberries

1 (5- or 6-ounce) package fresh baby spinach

1 (4-ounce) package chopped walnuts

1 (16-ounce) bottle light balsamic vinaigrette

1 (12.7-ounce) bottle dry sherry

1 (9-ounce) package refrigerated whole wheat 4-cheese ravioli

1 (12-ounce) package frozen pureed butternut squash

Check staples: 1% low-fat milk, ground nutmeg, salt, and black pepper

Menu

POINTS value: 7

Meatless Hash and Eggs

Citrus-Jícama Salad

Grocery List

1 (8-ounce) container prechopped tomato, green bell pepper, and onion mix

1 (24-ounce) jar red grapefruit sections

1 small jícama

1 small bunch fresh mint

1 (30-ounce) package frozen shredded hash brown potatoes

1 (12-ounce) package frozen meatless crumbles

Check staples: eggs, olive oil, cooking spray, ground cinnamon, salt, and black pepper

Meatless Hash and Eggs

prep: 3 minutes • **cook:** 16 minutes   *POINTS* value: 6

This meat-free dish, adapted from a traditional recipe for corned beef and hash, earned one of our Test Kitchen's highest ratings.

2½ cups frozen shredded hash brown potatoes
1½ cups frozen meatless crumbles
1½ cups prechopped tomato, green bell pepper, and onion mix
½ teaspoon salt
¼ teaspoon black pepper
 1 tablespoon olive oil
Cooking spray
 4 large eggs

1. Combine first 5 ingredients in a medium bowl.
2. Heat oil in a large nonstick skillet coated with cooking spray over medium heat. Add potato mixture, and cook 5 to 7 minutes or until potato mixture is thoroughly heated, stirring occasionally. Form 4 (3-inch) indentations in vegetable mixture using the back of a spoon. Break 1 egg into each indentation. Cover and cook 10 minutes or until eggs are done. Yield: 4 servings (serving size: 1 egg and 1 cup vegetable mixture).

Per serving: CALORIES 271 (36% from fat); FAT 10.8g (saturated fat 2.3g); PROTEIN 15.2g; CARBOHYDRATES 30.3g; FIBER 3.9g; CHOLESTEROL 212mg; IRON 3.4mg; SODIUM 527mg; CALCIUM 59mg

Citrus-Jícama Salad

prep: 9 minutes   *POINTS* value: 1

Drain 1 (24-ounce) jar red grapefruit sections, reserving ¼ cup juice. Combine juice, 2 tablespoons chopped fresh mint, and ⅛ teaspoon ground cinnamon in a medium bowl; stir with a whisk. Add grapefruit sections and ⅔ cup (1½-inch) matchstick-cut peeled jícama; toss gently. Yield: 4 servings (serving size: about ½ cup).

Per serving: CALORIES 91 (0% from fat); FAT 0g (saturated fat 0g); PROTEIN 1.6g; CARBOHYDRATES 21.1g; FIBER 2g; CHOLESTEROL 0mg; IRON 1mg; SODIUM 22mg; CALCIUM 9mg

Cheese and Green Onion Omelet

prep: 8 minutes • **cook:** 5 minutes   *POINTS* value: 5

This garden-fresh omelet for two is perfect for a brunch or simple supper. Top with your favorite marinara sauce, if desired.

3 large eggs
2 large egg whites
¾ cup finely chopped green onions
2 tablespoons 1% low-fat milk
½ teaspoon freshly ground black pepper
¼ teaspoon salt
Cooking spray
½ cup panko (Japanese breadcrumbs)
2 tablespoons shredded Italian cheese blend, divided
2 tablespoons chopped fresh parsley, divided

1. Combine first 6 ingredients in a medium bowl, stirring with a whisk.
2. Heat a large nonstick skillet over medium heat. Coat pan with cooking spray. Add bread-crumbs; cook 1 minute or until lightly browned. Pour egg mixture into pan. As mixture starts to cook, gently lift edges of omelet with a spatula, and tilt pan so uncooked portion flows underneath. Cook just until set (about 4 minutes).
3. Sprinkle half of cheese and parsley over omelet. Fold omelet in half; and cut in half cross-wise. Sprinkle top with remaining cheese and parsley. Serve immediately. Yield: 2 servings (serving size: ½ of omelet).

Per serving: CALORIES 224 (40% from fat); FAT 9.8g (saturated fat 3.3g); PROTEIN 18.2g; CARBOHYDRATES 15.1g; FIBER 1.7g; CHOLESTEROL 323mg; IRON 2.2mg; SODIUM 569mg; CALCIUM 145mg

Menu
POINTS value: 6

Cheese and Green Onion Omelet

1 cup red grapes ☑
POINTS value: 1

Grocery List

1 small bunch green onions

1 small bunch fresh parsley

1 pound seedless red grapes

1 (9-ounce) container panko (Japanese breadcrumbs)

1 (4-ounce) package shredded Italian cheese blend

Check staples: 1% low-fat milk, eggs, cooking spray, salt, and black pepper

Menu

POINTS value: 7

Sweet-and-Sour Tofu

1 cup prechopped
fresh pineapple ✓.
POINTS value: 1

Grocery List

1 large lemon

1 (10-ounce) package matchstick-cut carrots

1 (8-ounce) container prechopped celery, onion, and green bell pepper mix

1 (32-ounce) container prechopped fresh pineapple

1 (14-ounce) package water-packed firm tofu

1 (8-ounce) can no-salt-added tomato sauce

1 (8.8-ounce) package precooked whole-grain brown rice (such as Uncle Ben's)

Check staples: olive oil–flavored cooking spray, honey, salt, and black pepper

Sweet-and-Sour Tofu

prep: 2 minutes • **cook:** 13 minutes   *POINTS* value: 6

Use a mix of fresh prechopped celery, onion, and green bell pepper to speed up the preparation of this simple Chinese-style entrée.

  1 (8.8-ounce) package precooked whole-grain brown rice (such as Uncle Ben's)
  1 (14-ounce) package water-packed firm tofu, drained
    Olive oil–flavored cooking spray
  2 cups matchstick-cut carrots
1½ cups prechopped celery, onion, and green bell pepper mix
  1 (8-ounce) can no-salt-added tomato sauce
  3 tablespoons honey
  3 tablespoons fresh lemon juice
  ¼ teaspoon salt
  ¼ teaspoon freshly ground black pepper

1. Cook brown rice in microwave according to package directions; keep warm.

2. While rice cooks, place tofu on several layers of heavy-duty paper towels. Cover tofu with additional paper towels; gently press out moisture. Cut tofu into 1-inch cubes.

3. Heat a large nonstick skillet over medium-high heat. Coat pan with cooking spray. Add tofu; cook 3 to 4 minutes or until browned, stirring occasionally. Remove from pan; set aside, and keep warm.

4. Add carrots and prechopped vegetable mix to pan; sauté 4 minutes or until vegetables are tender. Stir in tomato sauce and next 4 ingredients. Cook 4 minutes or until mixture thickens, stirring constantly. Stir in reserved tofu. Serve immediately over rice. Yield: 4 servings (serving size: 1 cup tofu mixture and ½ cup rice).

Per serving: CALORIES 301 (20% from fat); FAT 6.8g (saturated fat 1.2g); PROTEIN 12.2g; CARBOHYDRATES 48.6g; FIBER 4.1g; CHOLESTEROL 0mg; IRON 2.4mg; SODIUM 212mg; CALCIUM 113mg

Meats

Grocery List

1 medium onion

1 large yellow squash

2 small zucchini

1 (10-ounce) can beef consommé

1 (8.8-ounce) package precooked long-grain white rice (such as Uncle Ben's)

1 pound ground sirloin

Check staples: olive oil, cooking spray, balsamic vinegar, dried Italian seasoning, Greek seasoning, salt, and black pepper

Hamburger Steak with Caramelized Onions

prep: 9 minutes • **cook:** 16 minutes   *POINTS* value: 4

These homestyle hamburgers are cooked in a savory onion gravy that keeps them juicy. Enjoy these smothered patties served over rice or mashed potatoes.

 1 pound ground sirloin
¼ teaspoon salt
¼ teaspoon black pepper
¼ teaspoon dried Italian seasoning
 Cooking spray
 1 medium onion, thinly sliced
½ cup beef consommé
¼ cup balsamic vinegar

1. Combine first 4 ingredients in a small bowl. Shape into 4 (½-inch-thick) patties.
2. Heat a large nonstick skillet over medium-high heat. Coat pan with cooking spray. Add patties; cook 3 to 4 minutes on each side or until browned. Transfer patties to a platter, and keep warm.
3. Add onion to pan; coat onion with cooking spray. Sauté over medium-high heat 4 minutes. Return patties to pan. Combine consommé and vinegar; pour over onion and patties. Bring mixture to a boil; reduce heat, cover, and simmer 5 to 6 minutes or until meat is done. Yield: 4 servings (serving size: 1 patty and 6 tablespoons onion mixture).

Per serving: CALORIES 163 (28% from fat); FAT 5g (saturated fat 2g); PROTEIN 23.7g; CARBOHYDRATES 6.3g; FIBER 0.8g; CHOLESTEROL 60mg; IRON 2.2mg; SODIUM 375mg; CALCIUM 17mg

Sautéed Summer Squash ☑.

prep: 3 minutes • **cook:** 5 minutes   *POINTS* value: 1

Heat 1 tablespoon olive oil in a large nonstick skillet over medium-high heat. Slice 2 small zucchini. Cut 1 large yellow squash in half lengthwise, and slice. Add vegetables to pan, and sprinkle with 1 teaspoon Greek seasoning. Cook 4 to 5 minutes or until lightly browned, stirring occasionally. Yield: 4 servings (serving size: ½ cup).

Per serving: CALORIES 48 (69% from fat); FAT 3.7g (saturated fat 0.5g); PROTEIN 1.1g; CARBOHYDRATES 3.7g; FIBER 1.5g; CHOLESTEROL 0mg; IRON 0.4mg; SODIUM 127mg; CALCIUM 18mg

pictured on page 121

Stuffed Peppers

prep: 4 minutes • **cook:** 10 minutes   *POINTS* value: 6

Make sure your peppers are 10 ounces or larger so the beef stuffing will fit.

- 2 large green bell peppers (about 10 ounces each)
- ¾ pound ground sirloin
- ¼ cup chopped onion
- 1 teaspoon dried Italian seasoning
- ¼ teaspoon salt
- ¼ teaspoon black pepper
- 1 (8.8-ounce) package precooked whole-grain brown rice (such as Uncle Ben's)
- 1 cup tomato-basil pasta sauce (such as Classico)
- 1 cup shredded part-skim mozzarella cheese

1. Cut bell peppers in half lengthwise; discard seeds and membranes. Place bell pepper halves, cut sides up, in an 11 x 7–inch baking dish. Microwave at HIGH 6 to 7 minutes or until tender.

2. While bell peppers cook, heat a large nonstick skillet over medium-high heat. Cook beef and onion until browned, stirring to crumble beef. Drain, if necessary; return to pan. Stir in dried Italian seasoning, salt, black pepper, brown rice, and pasta sauce. Cook 1 to 2 minutes or until warm, stirring occasionally.

3. Fill bell pepper halves with beef mixture; sprinkle evenly with cheese. Microwave at HIGH 2 to 3 minutes or until cheese melts. Yield: 4 servings (serving size: ½ pepper).

Per serving: CALORIES 312 (28% from fat); FAT 9.8g (saturated fat 4.6g); PROTEIN 27.4g; CARBOHYDRATES 29.9g; FIBER 4.1g; CHOLESTEROL 61mg; IRON 2.4mg; SODIUM 543mg; CALCIUM 242mg

Menu

POINTS value: 6

Stuffed Peppers

1 cup steamed yellow squash ☑.
POINTS **value: 0**

Grocery List

2 large green bell peppers (about 10 ounces each)

1 small onion

1 pound yellow squash

1 (26-ounce) jar tomato-basil pasta sauce (such as Classico)

1 (8.8-ounce) package precooked whole-grain brown rice (such as Uncle Ben's)

1 (4-ounce) package shredded part-skim mozzarella cheese

¾ pound ground sirloin

Check staples: dried Italian seasoning, salt, and black pepper

pictured on page 118

Menu

POINTS value: 6

Grilled Flank Steak with Chimichurri

Grilled Garlic Corn

1 cup sweet baby greens with red bell pepper, grape tomatoes, and balsamic vinaigrette ✓.
POINTS value: 0

Grocery List

1 small bunch fresh parsley

1 small bunch fresh mint

1 medium shallot

1 whole garlic head

1 small lemon

4 medium ears shucked corn

1 (4-ounce) package sweet baby greens

1 small red bell pepper

1 (16-ounce) container grape tomatoes

1 (3.5-ounce) jar capers

1 (8-ounce) bottle fat-free balsamic vinaigrette

1 pound flank steak

Check staples: olive oil, cooking spray, garlic salt, salt, and black pepper

Grilled Flank Steak with Chimichurri ✓.

prep: 9 minutes • **cook:** 6 minutes   *POINTS* value: 5

Chimichurri is a very flavorful, popular Argentine meat sauce composed of olive oil, parsley, garlic, and spices that commonly accompanies grilled meats. In our version, we've added salty capers and fresh lemon juice. You can make the sauce up to a day ahead and store it in the refrigerator.

  1 pound flank steak
  ¼ teaspoon freshly ground black pepper
  ⅛ teaspoon salt
  ½ cup chopped fresh parsley
  2 tablespoons chopped fresh mint
  2 tablespoons finely chopped shallots
  1 tablespoon capers
  1 tablespoon fresh lemon juice
  2 teaspoons olive oil
  1 garlic clove, minced

1. Prepare grill.

2. Sprinkle steak evenly with pepper and salt. Grill 3 to 4 minutes on each side, or until desired degree of doneness. Cut steak diagonally across grain into thin slices.

3. Combine parsley and next 6 ingredients in a small bowl. Serve over steak. Yield: 4 servings (serving size: 3 ounces steak and 2 tablespoons chimichurri).

Per serving: CALORIES 205 (47% from fat); FAT 10.5g (saturated fat 3.7g); PROTEIN 24.5g; CARBOHYDRATES 2.3g; FIBER 0.3g; CHOLESTEROL 40mg; IRON 2.4mg; SODIUM 202mg; CALCIUM 45mg

Grilled Garlic Corn ✓.

prep: 1 minute • **cook:** 12 minutes   *POINTS* value: 1

Prepare grill. Coat 4 medium ears shucked corn with cooking spray; sprinkle with ¼ teaspoon garlic salt and ¼ teaspoon freshly ground black pepper. Place corn on grill rack; cover and grill 6 minutes on each side or until slightly charred. Cut corn in half. Yield: 4 servings (serving size: 2 corn halves).

Per serving: CALORIES 78 (11% from fat); FAT 1.1g (saturated fat 0.2g); PROTEIN 2.9g; CARBOHYDRATES 17.2g; FIBER 2.5g; CHOLESTEROL 0mg; IRON 0.5mg; SODIUM 69mg; CALCIUM 2mg

Sirloin Steak with Red Wine Glaze

prep: 4 minutes • **cook:** 10 minutes • **other:** 8 hours   *POINTS* value: 3

Place the steak in the refrigerator to marinate before you leave for work. When you return home, your entire meal can be on the table in about 15 minutes.

⅔ cup dry red wine
1 tablespoon minced fresh rosemary
1 tablespoon Worcestershire sauce
¼ teaspoon salt, divided
¼ teaspoon freshly ground black pepper
1 pound boneless beef top sirloin steak
Cooking spray
1 tablespoon red currant jelly

1. Combine wine, rosemary, Worcestershire sauce, ⅛ teaspoon salt, and pepper in a large zip-top plastic bag. Add steak; seal bag, and marinate in refrigerator at least 8 hours.
2. Prepare grill.
3. Remove steak from bag, reserving marinade. Sprinkle steak with remaining ⅛ teaspoon salt.
4. Place steak on grill rack coated with cooking spray; cover and grill 5 to 6 minutes on each side or until desired degree of doneness.
5. While steak cooks, place reserved marinade in a medium saucepan; bring to a boil. Boil 4 minutes or until liquid reduces to ¼ cup; stir in jelly until smooth. Cut steak diagonally across grain into thin slices. Serve with sauce. Yield: 4 servings (serving size: 3 ounces steak and 1 tablespoon sauce).

Per serving: CALORIES 154 (26% from fat); FAT 4.5g (saturated fat 1.7g); PROTEIN 22.4g; CARBOHYDRATES 4.8g; FIBER 0.1g; CHOLESTEROL 42mg; IRON 1.9mg; SODIUM 236mg; CALCIUM 24mg

Horseradish Mashed Potatoes

prep: 2 minutes • **cook:** 3 minutes   *POINTS* value: 2

Measure 2 cups mashed potatoes from 1 (20-ounce) package refrigerated mashed potatoes (such as Simply Potatoes); reserve remaining potatoes for another use. Place potatoes in a microwave-safe bowl, and microwave at HIGH 3 minutes. Stir in 1 tablespoon yogurt-based spread (such as Brummel & Brown) and 2 teaspoons prepared horseradish. Yield: 4 servings (serving size: ½ cup).

Per serving: CALORIES 87 (25% from fat); FAT 2.4g (saturated fat 0.3g); PROTEIN 1.5g; CARBOHYDRATES 15.3g; FIBER 1.6g; CHOLESTEROL 0mg; IRON 0.3mg; SODIUM 308mg; CALCIUM 16mg

Menu

POINTS value: 5

Sirloin Steak with Red Wine Glaze

Horseradish Mashed Potatoes

½ cup steamed Brussels sprouts ☑

POINTS value: 0

Grocery List

1 small bunch fresh rosemary

1 pound Brussels sprouts

1 (5-ounce) bottle Worcestershire sauce

1 (4-ounce) jar prepared horseradish

1 (12-ounce) jar red currant jelly

1 (750-milliliter) bottle dry red wine

1 (20-ounce) package refrigerated mashed potatoes (such as Simply Potatoes)

1 (15-ounce) container yogurt-based spread (such as Brummel & Brown)

1 pound boneless beef top sirloin steak

Check staples: cooking spray, salt, and black pepper

Menu

POINTS value: 7

**Balsamic-Glazed Steaks
with Mushrooms**

**Lemon-Thyme
Grilled Asparagus**

½ cup roasted
red potato wedges ☑.

POINTS value: 1

Grocery List

4 medium portobello caps

1 small bunch fresh thyme

1 small lemon

1 pound asparagus spears

2 (8-ounce) beef strip steaks
(½ to ¾ inch thick)

1 (20-ounce) package refrigerated red potato wedges

Check staples: olive oil, olive
oil–flavored cooking spray,
balsamic vinegar, salt, and
black pepper

Balsamic-Glazed Steaks with Mushrooms

prep: 3 minutes • **cook:** 11 minutes   POINTS value: 5

Reducing the balsamic vinegar produces a rich syrup that adds a depth of flavor to the steak. Watch the vinegar carefully; it will burn quickly after 4 minutes of boiling.

½ cup balsamic vinegar
2 (8-ounce) beef strip steaks (½ to ¾ inch thick)
¾ teaspoon freshly ground black pepper, divided
⅜ teaspoon salt, divided
4 medium portobello caps
Olive oil–flavored cooking spray
1 teaspoon finely chopped fresh thyme

1. Prepare grill.
2. Bring vinegar to a boil in a medium saucepan over medium-high heat. Boil 3 to 4 minutes or until reduced to about 3 tablespoons.
3. Sprinkle steaks on both sides with ½ teaspoon pepper and ¼ teaspoon salt. Coat mushrooms with cooking spray. Place steaks and mushrooms on grill rack coated with cooking spray. Grill, covered, 4 minutes on each side or until steaks are desired degree of doneness and mushrooms are tender.
4. Brush both sides of steaks with 1 tablespoon reduced vinegar. Cut steaks in half. Thinly slice mushrooms; toss with thyme and remaining reduced vinegar, ¼ teaspoon pepper, and ⅛ teaspoon salt. Serve over steaks. Yield: 4 servings (serving size: 3 ounces steak and ¼ cup mushrooms).

Per serving: CALORIES 219 (32% from fat); FAT 7.4g (saturated fat 2.8g); PROTEIN 26.5g; CARBOHYDRATES 8.6g; FIBER 1.4g; CHOLESTEROL 67mg; IRON 2.6mg; SODIUM 300mg; CALCIUM 15mg

Lemon-Thyme Grilled Asparagus ☑.

prep: 3 minutes • **cook:** 4 minutes   POINTS value: 1

Prepare grill. Combine 1 tablespoon fresh lemon juice, 1 teaspoon chopped fresh thyme, 2 teaspoons olive oil, and ¼ teaspoon freshly ground black pepper in a medium bowl; stir with a whisk, and set aside. Trim 1 pound asparagus spears, and spray with olive oil–flavored cooking spray. Place on grill rack, and grill 4 minutes or until slightly tender. Add asparagus to lemon mixture, tossing gently to coat. Yield: 4 servings (serving size: ¼ of asparagus).

Per serving: CALORIES 37 (57% from fat); FAT 2.7g (saturated fat 0.4g); PROTEIN 1.4g; CARBOHYDRATES 3.1g; FIBER 1.2g; CHOLESTEROL 0mg; IRON 0.6mg; SODIUM 8mg; CALCIUM 15mg

pictured on page 44

Beef Tenderloin Steaks with Mushroom Gravy

prep: 3 minutes • **cook:** 12 minutes   *POINTS* value: 6

Tenderloin, the most tender cut of beef available, can be a bit pricey, but the melt-in-your-mouth results are worth the expense. Beef tenderloin steaks are often labeled "filet mignon."

　4　(4-ounce) beef tenderloin steaks, trimmed
　½　teaspoon freshly ground black pepper
　¼　teaspoon salt
　　　Cooking spray
　1　(8-ounce) package presliced baby portobello mushrooms
　½　cup minced shallots
　1　(1.25-ounce) package mushroom and herb gravy mix (such as McCormick)
　1　cup water

1. Sprinkle steaks with pepper and salt. Heat a large nonstick skillet over medium-high heat. Add steaks to pan, and cook 3 to 4 minutes on each side or until desired degree of doneness. Remove steaks from pan; keep warm.
2. Coat pan with cooking spray. Add mushrooms and shallots; cook 5 minutes. Empty gravy mix into a small bowl. Gradually add 1 cup water, stirring with a whisk until blended. Add gravy to pan, scraping pan to loosen browned bits. Cook 1 minute. Spoon gravy over steaks. Yield: 4 servings (serving size: 1 steak and ¼ cup gravy).

Per serving: CALORIES 252 (34% from fat); FAT 9.1g (saturated fat 3g); PROTEIN 28.1g; CARBOHYDRATES 11.4g; FIBER 1.1g; CHOLESTEROL 87mg; IRON 2.5mg; SODIUM 216mg; CALCIUM 45mg

Garlic Green Beans

prep: 2 minutes • **cook:** 8 minutes   *POINTS* value: 0

Microwave 1 (12-ounce) package pretrimmed green beans according to package directions. Melt 1 tablespoon light stick butter in a large nonstick skillet coated with cooking spray over medium heat. Add 1 cup grape tomatoes and 2 crushed garlic cloves; cook 1 minute, stirring constantly. Add green beans, ¼ teaspoon salt, and ¼ teaspoon freshly ground black pepper; cook 2 minutes or until thoroughly heated. Yield: 4 servings (serving size: ¾ cup).

Per serving: CALORIES 48 (27% from fat); FAT 1.7g (saturated fat 0.9g); PROTEIN 2g; CARBOHYDRATES 8.4g; FIBER 3.4g; CHOLESTEROL 4mg; IRON 1mg; SODIUM 176mg; CALCIUM 38mg

Menu

POINTS value: 7

Beef Tenderloin Steaks with Mushroom Gravy

Garlic Green Beans

½ cup country-style mashed potatoes
POINTS **value: 1**

Grocery List

1 (8-ounce) package presliced baby portobello mushrooms

3 medium shallots

1 (12-ounce) package pretrimmed green beans

1 (16-ounce) container grape tomatoes

1 whole garlic head

1 (1.25-ounce) package mushroom and herb gravy mix (such as McCormick)

1 (24-ounce) package refrigerated country-style mashed potatoes (such as Simply Potatoes)

4 (4-ounce) beef tenderloin steaks

Check staples: light stick butter, cooking spray, salt, and black pepper

Menu

POINTS value: 10

Italian-Style Pot Roast
Parmesan Polenta

Grocery List

1 (8-ounce) package presliced mushrooms

1 medium onion

1 (14.5-ounce) can Italian-style stewed tomatoes

1 (6-ounce) can tomato paste

1 (14-ounce) can fat-free, less-sodium chicken broth

1 (17.6-ounce) package instant polenta

1 (8-ounce) wedge Parmesan cheese

1 (2½-pound) chuck roast

Check staples: cooking spray, salt, and black pepper

Italian-Style Pot Roast

prep: 4 minutes • **cook:** 8 hours, 8 minutes • **other:** 5 minutes   **POINTS** value: 8

The slow cooker helps make this hearty meal a weeknight supper that you'll prepare over and over again. Long, slow, moist heat is the key to transforming this chuck roast into a succulent, fork-tender dish.

  1 (2½-pound) chuck roast, trimmed
  ¾ teaspoon salt, divided
  ¼ teaspoon freshly ground black pepper, divided
    Cooking spray
  1 (8-ounce) package presliced mushrooms
  1 (14.5-ounce) can Italian-style stewed tomatoes
  1 medium onion, thinly sliced
  ⅓ cup tomato paste

1. Sprinkle roast with ½ teaspoon salt and ⅛ teaspoon pepper.
2. Heat a large nonstick skillet over medium-high heat. Coat pan with cooking spray. Add roast; cook 2 minutes on each side or until lightly browned. Remove and set aside.
3. Add mushrooms to pan; sauté 4 minutes or until browned.
4. Combine mushrooms, tomatoes, onion, tomato paste, and remaining ¼ teaspoon salt and ⅛ teaspoon pepper in a 6-quart slow cooker. Add roast. Cover and cook on LOW 8 hours or until beef is tender.
5. Remove roast to a serving platter. Cover and keep warm. Transfer sauce to a large measuring cup; let stand 5 minutes. Discard fat. Serve sauce with roast. Yield: 9 servings (serving size: about 3 ounces meat and about ⅓ cup sauce).

Per serving: CALORIES 339 (62% from fat); FAT 23.5g (saturated fat 9.5g); PROTEIN 23.4g; CARBOHYDRATES 7.5g; FIBER 1.6g; CHOLESTEROL 83mg; IRON 3.1mg; SODIUM 371mg; CALCIUM 29mg

Parmesan Polenta

prep: 3 minutes • **cook:** 6 minutes   **POINTS** value: 2

Place 1⅓ cups instant polenta and ¼ teaspoon freshly ground black pepper in a large saucepan. Gradually add 2¼ cups water and 1 (14-ounce) can fat-free, less-sodium chicken broth, stirring constantly with a whisk. Bring to a boil, and reduce heat to medium. Cook 3 to 4 minutes or until thick, stirring frequently. Stir in ⅓ cup freshly grated Parmesan cheese. Serve immediately. Yield: 9 servings (serving size: ½ cup).

Per serving: CALORIES 100 (11% from fat); FAT 1.2g (saturated fat 0.6g); PROTEIN 4.1g; CARBOHYDRATES 12.7g; FIBER 2.3g; CHOLESTEROL 3mg; IRON 0mg; SODIUM 185mg; CALCIUM 60mg

Grilled Lamb Chops with Cherry Port Sauce

prep: 3 minutes • cook: 16 minutes   *POINTS* value: 6

We've used port, a sweet fortified wine, to create a vibrant sauce for the chops. Its distinctive flavor is hard to match, but if you need a substitute, use a fruity red wine, such as a zinfandel. For a nonalcoholic alternative, use ⅔ cup pomegranate-cherry juice and ½ teaspoon sugar.

 8 (4-ounce) lamb loin chops, trimmed
 ½ teaspoon salt, divided
 ½ teaspoon freshly ground black pepper
 ⅔ cup tawny port
 1 teaspoon cornstarch
 1 teaspoon water
 ¾ cup frozen pitted dark sweet cherries
 1 teaspoon minced fresh thyme
 Cooking spray

1. Prepare grill.

2. Sprinkle lamb evenly with ¼ teaspoon salt and pepper; set aside.

3. Bring port to a boil over high heat in a medium skillet. Boil, uncovered, 2 to 3 minutes or until reduced to ⅓ cup. Combine cornstarch and water, stirring until smooth. Reduce heat to medium. Add cornstarch mixture and cherries to pan. Simmer 1 minute or until sauce is slightly thick. Remove from heat; stir in thyme and remaining ¼ teaspoon salt.

4. Coat lamb with cooking spray; place on grill rack. Grill 5 minutes on each side or to desired degree of doneness. Serve cherry sauce over lamb. Yield: 4 servings (serving size: 2 chops and about 2½ tablespoons sauce).

Per serving: CALORIES 295 (28% from fat); FAT 9.3g (saturated fat 3.3g); PROTEIN 28.9g; CARBOHYDRATES 11.2g; FIBER 0.9g; CHOLESTEROL 91mg; IRON 2.1mg; SODIUM 374mg; CALCIUM 28mg

Grilled Red Onion and Zucchini ☑

prep: 2 minutes • cook: 10 minutes   *POINTS* value: 1

Prepare grill. Cut 1 large red onion into 4 (½-inch) slices and 2 large zucchini in half lengthwise. Combine 3 tablespoons balsamic vinegar, 2 teaspoons olive oil, and ¾ teaspoon Greek seasoning; brush over vegetables. Place vegetables on grill rack coated with cooking spray; cover and grill 10 to 12 minutes or until vegetables are tender. Yield: 4 servings (serving size: 1 zucchini half and 1 onion slice).

Per serving: CALORIES 68 (36% from fat); FAT 2.7g (saturated fat 0.4g); PROTEIN 2.4g; CARBOHYDRATES 10.4g; FIBER 2.4g; CHOLESTEROL 0mg; IRON 0.6mg; SODIUM 202mg; CALCIUM 33mg

Menu

POINTS value: 7

Grilled Lamb Chops with Cherry Port Sauce

Grilled Red Onion and Zucchini

Grocery List

1 large red onion

2 large zucchini

1 small bunch fresh thyme

1 (750-milliliter) bottle tawny port

1 (12-ounce) package frozen pitted dark sweet cherries

8 (4-ounce) lamb loin chops

Check staples: olive oil, cooking spray, balsamic vinegar, cornstarch, Greek seasoning, salt, and black pepper

Grocery List

1 small bunch fresh mint

1 small bunch fresh parsley

1 small lemon

1 plum tomato

1 whole garlic head

1 (7.6-ounce) box uncooked wheat couscous (such as Near East)

1 (6-ounce) carton plain fat-free yogurt

8 (4-ounce) lamb loin chops

Check staples: olive oil, cooking spray, salt, and black pepper

Lamb Chops with Minted Yogurt Sauce

prep: 4 minutes • **cook:** 6 minutes   *POINTS* value: 5

Tender lamb loin chops dressed up with a tangy, creamy dipping sauce and served with Couscous Salad make an attractive presentation that will impress your family and guests.

½ cup plain fat-free yogurt
 1 tablespoon chopped fresh mint
 1 teaspoon lemon juice
 1 small garlic clove, minced
½ teaspoon salt, divided
½ teaspoon freshly ground black pepper, divided
 8 (4-ounce) lamb loin chops, trimmed
Cooking spray

1. Prepare grill.

2. Combine yogurt and next 3 ingredients. Stir in ⅛ teaspoon salt and ⅛ teaspoon pepper. Chill.

3. Sprinkle lamb evenly with remaining ⅜ teaspoon each salt and pepper. Place lamb on grill rack coated with cooking spray; grill 3 minutes on each side or until desired degree of doneness. Serve with yogurt sauce. Yield: 4 servings (serving size: 2 chops and 2 table-spoons sauce).

Per serving: CALORIES 221 (38% from fat); FAT 9.3g (saturated fat 3.3g); PROTEIN 29.9g; CARBOHYDRATES 3g; FIBER 0.1g; CHOLESTEROL 91mg; IRON 2mg; SODIUM 388mg; CALCIUM 59mg

Couscous Salad

prep: 6 minutes • **cook:** 3 minutes • **other:** 5 minutes   *POINTS* value: 2

Bring ½ cup water to a boil in a small saucepan. Stir in ½ cup uncooked wheat couscous (such as Near East). Cover, remove from heat, and let stand 5 minutes. While couscous stands, combine ¾ cup chopped seeded plum tomato, ⅓ cup minced fresh parsley, ⅓ cup minced fresh mint, 2 tablespoons lemon juice, 1 tablespoon olive oil, and ⅛ teaspoon salt in a small bowl. Add couscous, and stir to combine. Serve at room temperature or chilled. Yield: 4 servings (serving size: ½ cup).

Per serving: CALORIES 110 (34% from fat); FAT 4.2g (saturated fat 0.5g); PROTEIN 3.2g; CARBOHYDRATES 16.6g; FIBER 1.9g; CHOLESTEROL 0mg; IRON 0.7mg; SODIUM 78mg; CALCIUM 16mg

Asian Pork Lettuce Wraps

prep: 8 minutes • **cook:** 7 minutes   *POINTS* value: 6

You'll love the freshly squeezed taste the crystallized lime gives to these lettuce wraps. Its tangy overtones balance the heat of the spicy chili garlic sauce. Look for crystallized lime alongside powdered beverage mixes at your supermarket.

Cooking spray
1   pound lean ground pork
4   packets crystallized lime (such as True Lime)
1   cup sliced green onions
2   tablespoons chili garlic sauce
4   large iceberg lettuce leaves
¼   cup chopped dry-roasted peanuts
Chili garlic sauce (optional)

1. Heat a large nonstick skillet over medium-high heat. Coat pan with cooking spray. Add pork; cook 6 minutes or until pork is browned, stirring to crumble. Add crystallized lime, green onions, and 2 tablespoons chili garlic sauce; cook 1 minute. Spoon pork mixture evenly onto center of lettuce leaves; sprinkle with peanuts, and roll up. Serve with additional chili garlic sauce, if desired. Yield: 4 servings (serving size: 1 wrap).

Per serving: CALORIES 246 (54% from fat); FAT 14.8g (saturated fat 4.7g); PROTEIN 25.1g; CARBOHYDRATES 5g; FIBER 1.6g; CHOLESTEROL 85mg; IRON 0.6mg; SODIUM 246mg; CALCIUM 26mg

Sesame Ginger Asian Slaw

prep: 8 minutes   *POINTS* value: 1

Combine 2 cups shredded Napa cabbage, 1 cup thinly sliced English cucumber, ½ cup thinly sliced radish, ½ cup matchstick-cut carrots, and ¼ cup light sesame ginger dressing (such as Newman's Own) in a medium bowl, tossing gently. Yield: 4 servings (serving size: about ¾ cup).

Per serving: CALORIES 36 (20% from fat); FAT 0.8g (saturated fat 0g); PROTEIN 0.9g; CARBOHYDRATES 6.5g; FIBER 1.3g; CHOLESTEROL 0mg; IRON 0.2mg; SODIUM 216mg; CALCIUM 42mg

Menu

POINTS value: 8

Asian Pork Lettuce Wraps

**Sesame Ginger
Asian Slaw**

1 large orange ☑.
***POINTS* value: 1**

Grocery List

1 small bunch green onions

1 large head iceberg lettuce

1 small head Napa cabbage

1 small English cucumber

1 small bunch radishes

1 (10-ounce) package matchstick-cut carrots

4 large oranges

1 (16-ounce) jar dry-roasted peanuts

1 (16-ounce) bottle light sesame ginger dressing (such as Newman's Own)

1 (10.7-ounce) bottle chili garlic sauce

1 (0.49-ounce) box crystallized lime (such as True Lime)

1 pound lean ground pork

Check staples: cooking spray

Menu

POINTS value: 8

Pork Chops with Caponata

Minted Orange Couscous

Grocery List

1 small bunch fresh basil

1 small bunch fresh mint

1 small orange

1 (4.5-ounce) bottle minced garlic

1 (7-ounce) can caponata (such as Alessi)

1 (14-ounce) can fat-free, less-sodium chicken broth

1 (9-ounce) container panko (Japanese breadcrumbs)

1 (10-ounce) box uncooked plain couscous

4 (4-ounce) boneless center-cut loin pork chops (½ inch thick)

Check staples: olive oil, olive oil–flavored cooking spray, balsamic vinegar, salt, and black pepper

Pork Chops with Caponata

prep: 6 minutes • **cook:** 9 minutes   **POINTS** value: 6

Caponata—a Sicilian dish made of eggplant, onions, olives, and tomatoes—is served at room temperature as an appetizer, salad, or side dish, or as a relish for meat and poultry. Look for it alongside the canned vegetables at your supermarket.

⅔ cup canned caponata (such as Alessi), chopped
2 tablespoons minced fresh basil
2 teaspoons balsamic vinegar
4 (4-ounce) boneless center-cut loin pork chops (½ inch thick)
¼ teaspoon salt
¼ teaspoon freshly ground black pepper
½ cup panko (Japanese breadcrumbs)
2 teaspoons olive oil
Olive oil–flavored cooking spray

1. Combine first 3 ingredients; set aside.
2. Sprinkle pork evenly with salt and pepper; dredge in breadcrumbs, pressing to adhere.
3. Heat oil in a large nonstick skillet coated with cooking spray over medium-high heat until hot. Add pork to pan. Cook 4 to 5 minutes on each side or until browned and done. Serve caponata mixture over pork. Yield: 4 servings (serving size: 1 chop and about 2 tablespoons caponata mixture).

Per serving: CALORIES 260 (46% from fat); FAT 13.3g (saturated fat 3.2g); PROTEIN 25.6g; CARBOHYDRATES 7.5g; FIBER 2.7g; CHOLESTEROL 65mg; IRON 1.6mg; SODIUM 372mg; CALCIUM 27mg

Minted Orange Couscous

prep: 5 minutes • **cook:** 3 minutes • **other:** 5 minutes   **POINTS** value: 2

Bring 1 cup fat-free, less-sodium chicken broth; ½ teaspoon bottled minced garlic; and ¼ teaspoon freshly ground black pepper to a boil in a medium saucepan. Gradually stir in ¾ cup uncooked plain couscous. Remove from heat; cover and let stand 5 minutes. Stir in 1 tablespoon chopped fresh mint and ½ teaspoon grated orange rind. Fluff with a fork. Yield: 4 servings (serving size: ½ cup).

Per serving: CALORIES 129 (2% from fat); FAT 0.3g (saturated fat 0.1g); PROTEIN 4.9g; CARBOHYDRATES 25.7g; FIBER 1.7g; CHOLESTEROL 0mg; IRON 0.4mg; SODIUM 291mg; CALCIUM 10mg

Pork Chops with Mustard Cream Sauce

prep: 3 minutes • **cook:** 14 minutes   *POINTS* value: 4

Using fat-free half-and-half gives this dish a creamy, rich flavor that fat-free milk can't. Sprinkle the finished dish with chopped fresh parsley, if desired.

  4 (4-ounce) boneless center-cut loin pork chops (½ inch thick)
  ½ teaspoon salt
  ¼ teaspoon black pepper
    Cooking spray
  ½ cup fat-free, less-sodium chicken broth
  ⅔ cup fat-free half-and-half
  1 tablespoon Dijon mustard
  2 teaspoons lemon juice
    Chopped fresh parsley (optional)

1. Sprinkle both sides of pork with salt and pepper.
2. Heat a large nonstick skillet over medium-high heat. Coat pan with cooking spray. Add pork, and cook 4 to 5 minutes on each side or until lightly browned and done. Transfer pork to a serving plate, and keep warm.
3. Add broth to pan, scraping pan to loosen browned bits. Stir in half-and-half, mustard, and lemon juice. Reduce heat, and simmer, uncovered, 6 minutes or until sauce is slightly thick. Spoon sauce over pork; sprinkle with parsley, if desired. Yield: 4 servings (serving size: 1 chop and 2 tablespoons sauce).

Per serving: CALORIES 193 (30% from fat); FAT 6.4g (saturated fat 2.3g); PROTEIN 24.3g; CARBOHYDRATES 5.2g; FIBER 0g; CHOLESTEROL 65mg; IRON 0.7mg; SODIUM 539mg; CALCIUM 52mg

White Beans and Bacon

prep: 5 minutes • **cook:** 9 minutes   *POINTS* value: 2

Heat a large nonstick skillet over medium heat until hot. Chop 2 slices lower-sodium bacon. Add bacon to pan, and cook 3 minutes or until bacon begins to brown, stirring often. Stir in 1 cup chopped onion, and cook 4 minutes or until onion is tender, stirring often. Rinse and drain 1 (15-ounce) can no-salt-added cannellini beans (such as Eden); add beans, ¼ teaspoon salt, and ¼ teaspoon black pepper to pan. Cook 2 minutes or just until thoroughly heated. Yield: 4 cups (serving size: ½ cup).

Per serving: CALORIES 122 (39% from fat); FAT 5.4g (saturated fat 1.7g); PROTEIN 5.2g; CARBOHYDRATES 13.7g; FIBER 4.2g; CHOLESTEROL 8mg; IRON 1.5mg; SODIUM 249mg; CALCIUM 50mg

---

Menu

POINTS value: 6

Pork Chops with Mustard Cream Sauce

White Beans and Bacon

2 tomato slices
POINTS value: 0

Grocery List

1 small lemon

1 small bunch fresh parsley (optional)

1 small onion

2 large tomatoes

1 (14-ounce) can fat-free, less-sodium chicken broth

1 (15-ounce) can no-salt-added cannellini beans (such as Eden)

1 (16-ounce) carton fat-free half-and-half

4 (4-ounce) boneless center-cut loin pork chops (½ inch thick)

1 (16-ounce) package lower-sodium bacon

Check staples: cooking spray, Dijon mustard, salt, and black pepper

Menu:

POINTS value: 4

Chili-Caramelized Pork Medallions

Orange Asparagus

Grocery List

1 pound asparagus spears

1 large orange

1 (15-ounce) bottle citrus stir-fry sauce (such as Iron Chef Orange Sauce Glaze with Ginger)

1 (1-pound) pork tenderloin

Check staples: canola oil, cooking spray, chili powder, salt, and black pepper

Chili-Caramelized Pork Medallions

prep: 5 minutes • **cook:** 9 minutes   *POINTS* value: 4

The meat is cooked in two batches so that it browns quickly and remains moist and tender.

  1 (1-pound) pork tenderloin, trimmed and cut crosswise into ½-inch-thick slices
1½ teaspoons chili powder
¼ teaspoon salt
  2 teaspoons canola oil
  Cooking spray
⅓ cup citrus stir-fry sauce (such as Iron Chef Orange Sauce Glaze with Ginger)

1. Sprinkle pork on both sides with chili powder and salt.
2. Heat oil in a large nonstick skillet coated with cooking spray. Add half of pork, and cook 2 to 3 minutes on each side or until browned. Remove pork; keep warm. Repeat with remaining pork. Return pork to pan; add sauce, and cook 30 seconds, turning pork in sauce to coat. Yield: 4 servings (serving size: 3 ounces).

Per serving: CALORIES 176 (40% from fat); FAT 7.9g (saturated fat 1.7g); PROTEIN 23.8g; CARBOHYDRATES 1g; FIBER 0g; CHOLESTEROL 74mg; IRON 1.4mg; SODIUM 285mg; CALCIUM 5.8mg

Orange Asparagus

prep: 3 minutes • **cook:** 6 minutes   *POINTS* value: 0

Cut 1 pound asparagus spears into 1½-inch pieces. Cook in boiling water 4 minutes or until crisp-tender. Drain; return asparagus to pan. Add 2 teaspoons grated orange rind, ¼ cup fresh orange juice, ¼ teaspoon salt, and ¼ teaspoon freshly ground black pepper. Toss gently. Serve immediately. Yield: 4 servings (serving size: 1 cup).

Per serving: CALORIES 39 (0% from fat); FAT 0g (saturated fat 0g); PROTEIN 2.6g; CARBOHYDRATES 6.8g; FIBER 2.6g; CHOLESTEROL 0mg; IRON 0.5mg; SODIUM 144mg; CALCIUM 28mg

pictured on page 40

Chutney-Glazed Curry Pork Tenderloin

prep: 2 minutes • **cook:** 30 minutes • **other:** 5 minutes   *POINTS* value: 4

Keep a jar of chutney on hand as an easy way to add a kick to meats and poultry. Cook both the pork and roasted carrots on the same baking rack in the oven at the same time.

  1 tablespoon curry powder
  ¼ teaspoon crushed red pepper
  1 garlic clove, minced
  1 pound pork tenderloin
  ½ cup mango chutney

1. Preheat oven to 425°.
2. Combine first 3 ingredients in a small bowl. Place pork in a 13 x 9–inch baking pan; rub evenly with spice mixture. Bake at 425° for 10 minutes.
3. Baste pork with half of chutney. Bake an additional 20 minutes or until thermometer registers 155° or desired degree of doneness, basting with remaining chutney after 10 minutes. Let stand 5 minutes, and cut into slices. Yield: 4 servings (serving size: about 3 ounces).

Per serving: CALORIES 195 (20% from fat); FAT 4.3g (saturated fat 1.4g); PROTEIN 24.5g; CARBOHYDRATES 14.6g; FIBER 1.3g; CHOLESTEROL 74mg; IRON 2.2mg; SODIUM 64mg; CALCIUM 25mg

Roasted Carrots ☑.

prep: 2 minutes • **cook:** 20 minutes   *POINTS* value: 1

Combine 1 pound baby carrots, 2 teaspoons olive oil, ½ teaspoon chopped fresh thyme, ¼ teaspoon kosher salt, and ¼ teaspoon freshly ground black pepper in a jelly-roll pan coated with cooking spray. Bake at 425° for 20 to 25 minutes or until carrots are lightly browned and tender. Yield: 4 servings (serving size: about ⅔ cup).

Per serving: CALORIES 60 (38% from fat); FAT 2.5g (saturated fat 0.4g); PROTEIN 0.8g; CARBOHYDRATES 9.5g; FIBER 3.3g; CHOLESTEROL 0mg; IRON 1mg; SODIUM 206mg; CALCIUM 37mg

---

Menu
POINTS value: 7

Chutney-Glazed Curry Pork Tenderloin

Roasted Carrots

½ cup white rice with chopped green onions
POINTS value: 2

Grocery List

1 whole garlic head

1 (1-pound) package baby carrots

1 small bunch fresh thyme

1 small bunch green onions

1 (15-ounce) jar mango chutney

1 (8.8-ounce) package precooked long-grain white rice

1 pound pork tenderloin

Check staples: olive oil, cooking spray, curry powder, crushed red pepper, kosher salt, and black pepper

Menu

POINTS value: 7

Bacon and Sun-Dried Tomato Alfredo Pasta

Romaine and Mushroom Salad

Grocery List

1 small bunch fresh basil

1 (10-ounce) package torn romaine lettuce

1 (8-ounce) package presliced mushrooms

1 small English cucumber

1 small tomato

1 (3-ounce) package sun-dried tomatoes, packed without oil

1 (8-ounce) bottle fat-free balsamic vinaigrette

1 (14.5-ounce) package multi-grain penne (such as Barilla Plus)

1 (10-ounce) package light Alfredo sauce

1 (2.1-ounce) package precooked bacon

Check staples: black pepper

Bacon and Sun-Dried Tomato Alfredo Pasta

prep: 1 minute • **cook:** 14 minutes   **POINTS value: 7**

A rich, creamy sauce coats the fiber-rich multigrain pasta in this one-dish meal, and the smokiness from the bacon heightens the flavor. Toss the ingredients for the salad while the pasta cooks to keep your kitchen time short.

    8 ounces uncooked multigrain penne (such as Barilla Plus)
    1 (10-ounce) package light Alfredo sauce
    ½ cup sun-dried tomatoes, packed without oil and cut into julienne strips
    4 slices precooked bacon
    ¼ cup chopped fresh basil
    ¼ teaspoon freshly ground black pepper

1. Cook pasta according to package directions, omitting salt and fat; drain and keep warm.
2. While pasta cooks, combine Alfredo sauce and sun-dried tomatoes in a saucepan. Cook over low heat 6 to 8 minutes or until thoroughly heated and tomatoes are juicy and plump, stirring occasionally. While sauce cooks, microwave bacon according to package directions. Crumble bacon, and set aside.
3. Combine cooked pasta and Alfredo sauce mixture in a large serving bowl. Top with crumbled bacon, basil, and black pepper. Yield: 4 servings (serving size: 1 cup).

Per serving: CALORIES 337 (23% from fat); FAT 8.7g (saturated fat 4.8g); PROTEIN 17.5g; CARBOHYDRATES 48.2g; FIBER 5g; CHOLESTEROL 28mg; IRON 2.5mg; SODIUM 670mg; CALCIUM 148mg

Romaine and Mushroom Salad ✅

prep: 2 minutes   **POINTS value: 0**

Combine 3 cups torn romaine lettuce, ½ cup presliced mushrooms, ½ cup sliced English cucumber, ½ cup chopped tomato, and ⅓ cup fat-free balsamic vinaigrette in a large bowl; toss well. Yield: 4 servings (serving size: about 1 cup).

Per serving: CALORIES 33 (5% from fat); FAT 0.2g (saturated fat 0g); PROTEIN 1.2g; CARBOHYDRATES 7.1g; FIBER 1.4g; CHOLESTEROL 0mg; IRON 0.6mg; SODIUM 272mg; CALCIUM 19mg

Chocolate-Almond
Ice Cream Cake, *page 53*

Shrimp, Avocado, and
Corn Salad, *page 151*

Thai Green Curry Chicken,
page 132

Mini White Pizzas with Vegetables, *page 92*

Beef and Vegetable
Soup, *page 181*

Grilled Flank Steak with Chimichurri, *page 100*

Teriyaki Salmon with
Mushrooms, *page 77*

Chicken Thighs with
Chipotle-Peach Sauce,
page 141

Stuffed Peppers,
page 99

Honey Barbecue Chicken
Sandwiches, *page 170*

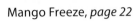
Mango Freeze, *page 22*

Lemon-Parsley Chicken,
page 138

Black Bean and Spinach
Quesadillas, *page 89*

Blackberry-Almond Cheesecake
Tarts, *page 59*

126

Grilled Thai-Spiced Chicken, *page 136*

Cherry Turnovers,
page 58

Poultry

Grocery List

1 (16-ounce) container refrigerated fresh salsa

1 small jalapeño pepper

1 small bunch fresh cilantro

1 (7-ounce) package baby lettuce mix with vegetables (such as Fresh Express Veggie Spring Mix)

1 medium tomato

1 (2-pound) rotisserie chicken

1 (8-ounce) bottle light ranch dressing

1 (6¾-ounce) bag light tortilla chips (such as Tostitos Light Restaurant Style)

1 (8-ounce) package preshredded reduced-fat 4-cheese Mexican blend cheese

1 (8-ounce) carton reduced-fat sour cream

Check staples: cooking spray

Cheesy Chicken Nachos

prep: 8 minutes • **cook:** 5 minutes   *POINTS* value: 7

Nachos, typically a south-of-the-border appetizer, make a satisfying and easy dinner when combined with a garden salad. Our version features a store-bought rotisserie chicken, but cooked chicken breast would work well, too.

  1 (6¾-ounce) bag light tortilla chips (such as Tostitos Light Restaurant Style)
Cooking spray
  2 cups shredded roasted chicken breast
  1 cup (4 ounces) preshredded reduced-fat 4-cheese Mexican blend cheese
  1 cup refrigerated fresh salsa
  ½ cup reduced-fat sour cream
  1 jalapeño pepper, minced
  ⅓ cup chopped fresh cilantro

1. Preheat oven to 400°.

2. Arrange tortilla chips in a single layer on a baking sheet lined with foil. Coat foil with cooking spray. Sprinkle chips evenly with chicken and cheese. Bake at 400° for 5 minutes or until cheese melts. Top evenly with salsa, sour cream, jalapeño, and cilantro. Serve immediately. Yield: 5 servings (serving size: about 10 chips).

Per serving: CALORIES 327 (28% from fat); FAT 10g (saturated fat 4.9g); PROTEIN 27.8g; CARBOHYDRATES 30.8g; FIBER 1.5g; CHOLESTEROL 68mg; IRON 1.1mg; SODIUM 648mg; CALCIUM 266mg

Green Salad with Veggies

prep: 4 minutes   *POINTS* value: 1

Combine 1 (7-ounce) package baby lettuce mix with vegetables (such as Fresh Express Veggie Spring Mix) and 1¼ cups chopped tomato in a large bowl; drizzle with 5 tablespoons light ranch dressing, and toss well. Yield: 5 servings (serving size: about 1½ cups).

Per serving: CALORIES 56 (56% from fat); FAT 3.5g (saturated fat 0.3g); PROTEIN 1.5g; CARBOHYDRATES 5.7g; FIBER 1.6g; CHOLESTEROL 4mg; IRON 0.7mg; SODIUM 170mg; CALCIUM 27mg

Green Chile and Chicken Tostadas

prep: 3 minutes • cook: 11 minutes   *POINTS* value: 7

This baked tostada features canned green salsa made from tangy tomatillos and spicy serrano peppers. Serve the leftover salsa with the Fiesta Tortilla Chips on page 182 for a quick snack, or as a condiment for burritos, tacos, or quesadillas.

 4 (6-inch) flour tortillas
Cooking spray
 2 cups chopped roasted chicken breast
 ½ cup green salsa (such as Herdez Salsa Verde)
 ½ cup (2 ounces) reduced-fat shredded Cheddar cheese
 ¾ cup preshredded lettuce
 1 tomato, chopped
 4 tablespoons reduced-fat sour cream

1. Preheat oven to 425°.
2. Lightly coat flour tortillas on both sides with cooking spray. Place tortillas on a baking sheet coated with cooking spray. Bake at 425° for 10 minutes or until crisp and golden, turning once.
3. While tortillas cook, place chicken in a small microwave-safe bowl. Microwave at HIGH 1 minute or until warm.
4. Spread 2 tablespoons salsa, ½ cup chicken, and 2 tablespoons cheese over each tortilla. Return to oven; broil 1 minute or until cheese melts.
5. Top tortillas evenly with lettuce, tomato, and sour cream. Serve immediately. Yield: 4 servings (serving size: 1 tostada).

Per serving: CALORIES 300 (31% from fat); FAT 10.2g (saturated fat 4.7g); PROTEIN 29.3g; CARBOHYDRATES 21.7g; FIBER 1.6g; CHOLESTEROL 78mg; IRON 2mg; SODIUM 787mg; CALCIUM 190mg

Menu

POINTS value: 8

Green Chile and Chicken Tostadas

1 cup mixed melon and pineapple ✓.
POINTS value: 1

Grocery List

1 (8-ounce) package preshredded lettuce

1 large tomato

1 (32-ounce) container pre-chopped melon and pineapple mix

1 (11.3-ounce) package (6-inch) flour tortillas

1 (2-pound) rotisserie chicken

1 (7-ounce) can green salsa (such as Herdez Salsa Verde)

1 (8-ounce) package reduced-fat shredded Cheddar cheese

1 (8-ounce) carton reduced-fat sour cream

Check staples: cooking spray

Thai Green Curry Chicken

prep: 2 minutes • **cook:** 10 minutes

POINTS value: 3

Menu

POINTS value: 7

Thai Green Curry Chicken

Cucumber, Pineapple, and Mint Salad

¾ cup jasmine rice with chopped red bell pepper and cilantro
POINTS value: 3

Grocery List

1 medium onion

1 small bunch fresh cilantro

1 small bunch fresh mint

1 small lime (optional)

1 peeled and cored pineapple

1 medium cucumber

1 small bunch green onions

1 small red bell pepper

1 (2-pound) rotisserie chicken

1 (14-ounce) can fat-free, less-sodium chicken broth

1 (13.5-ounce) can light coconut milk

1 (4-ounce) jar green curry paste

1 (7-ounce) bottle fish sauce

1 (12-ounce) bottle seasoned rice vinegar

1 (14-ounce) box uncooked boil-in-bag jasmine rice

Check staples: cooking spray

Creamy coconut milk and spicy curry paste provide authentic Thai flavor to this quick entrée. Both ingredients can be found in the international-foods section at your local supermarket. Serve over fragrant jasmine rice to soak up the sauce.

Cooking spray
1 medium onion, halved and vertically sliced
2 teaspoons green curry paste
2 cups thinly sliced roasted chicken breast
1 cup fat-free, less-sodium chicken broth
⅔ cup light coconut milk
3 tablespoons chopped fresh cilantro
Lime wedges (optional)
Cilantro sprigs (optional)

1. Heat a large nonstick skillet over medium-high heat. Coat pan with cooking spray. Add onion, and sauté 5 minutes; stir in curry paste. Add chicken, broth, and coconut milk to pan; bring to a boil. Reduce heat, and simmer 3 minutes. Spoon into bowls; sprinkle evenly with cilantro. Serve with lime wedges and garnish with a sprig of cilantro, if desired. Yield: 4 servings (serving size: 1 cup chicken mixture).

Per serving: CALORIES 155 (26% from fat); FAT 4.5g (saturated fat 2.6g); PROTEIN 23.2g; CARBOHYDRATES 5.1g; FIBER 0.8g; CHOLESTEROL 60mg; IRON 1.1mg; SODIUM 457mg; CALCIUM 21mg

Cucumber, Pineapple, and Mint Salad ☑

prep: 5 minutes

POINTS value: 1

Combine 1 coarsely chopped medium cucumber, 1 cup coarsely chopped pineapple, 2 thinly sliced green onions, 3 tablespoons chopped fresh mint, 1 tablespoon seasoned rice vinegar, and 1 tablespoon fish sauce in a medium bowl; toss well. Chill until ready to serve. Yield: 4 servings (serving size: ¾ cup).

Per serving: CALORIES 37 (2% from fat); FAT 0.1g (saturated fat 0g); PROTEIN 1.4g; CARBOHYDRATES 8.5g; FIBER 1.1g; CHOLESTEROL 0mg; IRON 0.6mg; SODIUM 424mg; CALCIUM 30mg

Green Chile–Black Bean Chicken

prep: 3 minutes • **cook:** 9 minutes

POINTS value: 4

Microwave the rice before you begin cooking the entrée so both dishes will be ready at the same time. To serve, spoon the saucy chicken over the rice and top with sour cream.

Cooking spray
1½ pounds chicken breast tenders, sliced crosswise into bite-sized pieces
¾ cup prechopped onion
¼ teaspoon salt
¼ teaspoon freshly ground black pepper
1 (15-ounce) can black beans, rinsed and drained
1 cup grape tomatoes, halved
1 (4.5-ounce) can chopped green chiles, undrained
¼ cup chopped fresh cilantro
¼ cup reduced-fat sour cream

1. Place a large nonstick skillet over medium-high heat until hot. Coat pan with cooking spray.
2. Add chicken and onion to pan; coat with cooking spray, and sprinkle with salt and pepper. Cook 7 minutes or until done, stirring occasionally.
3. Add black beans, tomatoes, and green chiles. Cook 2 minutes, stirring occasionally, until thoroughly heated. Sprinkle cilantro over chicken mixture, and top with sour cream before serving. Yield: 4 servings (serving size: 1½ cups chicken mixture and 1 tablespoon sour cream).

Per serving: CALORIES 252 (10% from fat); FAT 2.7g (saturated fat 1.2g); PROTEIN 43.7g; CARBOHYDRATES 17.5g; FIBER 5.3g; CHOLESTEROL 108mg; IRON 2.5mg; SODIUM 475mg; CALCIUM 59mg

Yellow Rice ✓

prep: 1 minute • **cook:** 12 minutes

POINTS value: 2

Combine 4 cups water, ½ teaspoon salt, ½ teaspoon ground turmeric, and 1 bay leaf in a medium bowl. Add 1 (3½-ounce) bag boil-in-bag brown rice, pressing down into liquid to thoroughly moisten. Microwave, uncovered, at HIGH 12 to 13 minutes or until tender; drain well, discarding liquid. Cut bag open, and return rice to bowl; fluff with a fork. Yield: 4 servings (serving size: ½ cup).

Per serving: CALORIES 90 (5% from fat); FAT 0.5g (saturated fat 0g); PROTEIN 2.1g; CARBOHYDRATES 19.1g; FIBER 1.1g; CHOLESTEROL 0mg; IRON 0.4mg; SODIUM 156mg; CALCIUM 0mg

Menu

POINTS value: 6

Green Chile–Black Bean Chicken

Yellow Rice

Grocery List

1 (8-ounce) container pre-chopped onion

1 (16-ounce) container grape tomatoes

1 small bunch fresh cilantro

1 (15-ounce) can black beans

1 (4.5-ounce) can chopped green chiles

1 (14-ounce) box boil-in-bag brown rice

1 (8-ounce) carton reduced-fat sour cream

1½ pounds chicken breast tenders

Check staples: cooking spray, ground turmeric, bay leaf, salt, and black pepper

pictured on page 38

Chipotle-Yogurt Chicken Kebabs

prep: 6 minutes • **cook:** 11 minutes • **other:** 1 hour   *POINTS* value: 4

We used both the chiles and the sauce from a can of adobo chiles to give this menu a smoky and spicy flavor. Serve with grilled pineapple slices and cooked couscous tossed with chopped tomato, onion, and fresh parsley.

½   cup plain fat-free yogurt
1   chipotle chile in adobo sauce, minced
1   large garlic clove, crushed
1   teaspoon ground cumin
½   teaspoon salt
¼   teaspoon pepper
1½ pounds skinless, boneless chicken breasts, cut into 1-inch cubes
    Cooking spray

1. Combine first 6 ingredients in a small bowl, stirring with a whisk. Pour into a heavy-duty zip-top plastic bag. Add chicken; seal bag, and toss to coat. Marinate in refrigerator 1 to 2 hours, turning bag occasionally.
2. Prepare grill.
3. Thread chicken evenly onto 4 (10-inch) metal skewers; place on grill rack coated with cooking spray. Grill 11 minutes or until done, turning once. Yield: 4 servings (serving size: 1 kebab).

Per serving: CALORIES 206 (10% from fat); FAT 2.3g (saturated fat 0.6g); PROTEIN 40.7g; CARBOHYDRATES 3.4g; FIBER 0.2g; CHOLESTEROL 99mg; IRON 1.5mg; SODIUM 445mg; CALCIUM 64mg

Sweet-n-Spicy Grilled Pineapple

prep: 2 minutes • **cook:** 6 minutes   *POINTS* value: 1

Prepare grill. Cut a peeled and cored pineapple into 8 slices, reserving 1½ tablespoons juice. Combine pineapple juice, 3 tablespoons light brown sugar, and 1 tablespoon adobo sauce from canned chipotle chiles in a small bowl, stirring with a whisk until blended. Blot excess moisture from each pineapple slice with paper towels. Brush 1 side of each slice with brown sugar mixture. Place, brushed sides down, on grill rack coated with cooking spray. Grill 3 minutes or until browned; brush with remaining brown sugar mixture, turn, and grill 3 minutes. Yield: 4 servings (serving size: 2 pineapple slices).

Per serving: CALORIES 87 (2% from fat); FAT 0.2g (saturated fat 0g); PROTEIN 0.6g; CARBOHYDRATES 22.7g; FIBER 2g; CHOLESTEROL 0mg; IRON 0.5mg; SODIUM 45mg; CALCIUM 22mg

Menu

POINTS value: 7

Chipotle-Yogurt Chicken Kebabs

Sweet-n-Spicy Grilled Pineapple

½ cup couscous with tomato, onion, and parsley
POINTS value: 2

Grocery List

1 whole garlic head

1 peeled and cored pineapple

1 plum tomato

1 small onion

1 small bunch fresh parsley

1 (7.5-ounce) can chipotle chiles in adobo sauce

1 (10-ounce) box uncooked plain couscous

1 (6-ounce) carton plain fat-free yogurt

1½ pounds skinless, boneless chicken breasts

Check staples: cooking spray, light brown sugar, ground cumin, salt, and black pepper

Fig and Balsamic Chicken

prep: 6 minutes • **cook:** 18 minutes   ***POINTS*** value: 5

We used water to deglaze the pan and capture the browned bits of flavor remaining after the chicken had seared. Roast the potatoes while you prepare the entrée.

  4 (6-ounce) skinless, boneless chicken breast halves
½ teaspoon salt, divided
   Cooking spray
½ cup prechopped red onion
¼ cup water
⅓ cup fig preserves
  2 tablespoons balsamic vinegar
¼ teaspoon dried Italian seasoning
¼ teaspoon freshly ground black pepper

1. Place chicken breast halves between 2 sheets of heavy-duty plastic wrap; pound to ½-inch thickness using a meat mallet or small heavy skillet. Sprinkle chicken with ¼ teaspoon salt.
2. Heat a large nonstick skillet over medium-high heat until hot. Coat pan with cooking spray. Add onion; sauté 3 minutes. Add chicken to pan; cook 7 minutes on each side or until done. Remove chicken from pan; keep warm.
3. Add water to pan, scraping pan to loosen browned bits. Reduce heat to medium; add preserves, next 3 ingredients, and remaining ¼ teaspoon salt. Cook 1 minute or until preserves melt, stirring constantly. Spoon fig sauce over chicken, and serve immediately. Yield: 4 servings (serving size: 1 chicken breast half and 2 tablespoons sauce).

Per serving: CALORIES 263 (7% from fat); FAT 2.1g (saturated fat 0.6g); PROTEIN 39.6g; CARBOHYDRATES 18g; FIBER 0.4g; CHOLESTEROL 99mg; IRON 1.3mg; SODIUM 404mg; CALCIUM 26mg

Roasted Potato Wedges

prep: 3 minutes • **cook:** 20 minutes   ***POINTS*** value: 2

Preheat oven to 475°. Combine 1 pound quartered small red potatoes and 2 teaspoons olive oil in a medium bowl, tossing to coat. Combine ¼ cup panko (Japanese breadcrumbs) with Italian seasoning and 2 tablespoons grated Parmesan-Romano cheese blend in a large zip-top plastic bag; add potatoes, tossing to coat. Place potatoes on a jelly-roll pan coated with cooking spray; discard remaining breadcrumb mixture. Bake at 475° for 20 minutes or until browned and crispy. Yield: 4 servings (serving size: about ¾ cup).

Per serving: CALORIES 123 (26% from fat); FAT 3.7g (saturated fat 1.1g); PROTEIN 3.9g; CARBOHYDRATES 19.9g; FIBER 2.2g; CHOLESTEROL 4mg; IRON 0.9mg; SODIUM 88mg; CALCIUM 56mg

Menu

POINTS value: 7

Fig and Balsamic Chicken

Roasted Potato Wedges

¾ cup steamed green beans ☑.
    POINTS value: 0

Grocery List

1 (8-ounce) container pre-chopped red onion

1 pound small red potatoes

1 (12-ounce) package pre-trimmed green beans

1 (11.5-ounce) jar fig preserves

1 (9-ounce) container panko (Japanese breadcrumbs) with Italian seasoning

1 (3-ounce) container grated Parmesan-Romano cheese blend

4 (6-ounce) skinless, boneless chicken breast halves

Check staples: olive oil, cooking spray, balsamic vinegar, dried Italian seasoning, salt, and black pepper

pictured on page 127

Grilled Thai-Spiced Chicken

prep: 5 minutes • **cook:** 12 minutes   *POINTS* value: 4

The tangy cucumber salad and grilled sweet red bell pepper complement the fiery grilled chicken in this zesty menu.

Menu

POINTS value: 6

Grilled Thai-Spiced Chicken

Cucumber Salad

½ cup white rice with chopped green onions
POINTS value: 2

¾ cup grilled red bell pepper slices ☑.
POINTS value: 0

Grocery List

1 small bunch fresh cilantro

1 small bunch green onions

1 medium English cucumber

2 large red bell peppers

1 (4-ounce) jar red curry paste

1 (12-ounce) bottle seasoned rice vinegar

1 (10-ounce) bottle low-sodium soy sauce

1 (2.5-ounce) jar sesame seeds

1 (8.8-ounce) package precooked long-grain white rice (such as Uncle Ben's)

4 (6-ounce) skinless, boneless chicken breast halves

Check staples: cooking spray, sugar, salt, and black pepper

4 (6-ounce) skinless, boneless chicken breast halves
½ teaspoon salt
¼ teaspoon pepper
2 teaspoons red curry paste
Cooking spray
1 tablespoon chopped fresh cilantro

1. Prepare grill.

2. Sprinkle chicken with salt and pepper; spread each side of chicken breast halves with ¼ teaspoon curry paste.

3. Place chicken on grill rack coated with cooking spray. Cover and grill 6 minutes on each side or until done. Sprinkle with cilantro. Yield: 4 servings (serving size: 1 chicken breast half).

Per serving: CALORIES 191 (10% from fat); FAT 2.1g (saturated fat 0.6g); PROTEIN 39.3g; CARBOHYDRATES 0.8g; FIBER 0g; CHOLESTEROL 99mg; IRON 1.2mg; SODIUM 446mg; CALCIUM 20mg

Cucumber Salad

prep: 3 minutes   *POINTS* value: 0

Combine 3 tablespoons seasoned rice vinegar, 2 teaspoons low-sodium soy sauce, 1 teaspoon toasted sesame seeds, and ½ teaspoon sugar in a small bowl; set aside. Cut 1 medium English cucumber in half crosswise. Use a vegetable peeler to cut cucumber lengthwise into thin strips to form ribbons. Discard cucumber peel. Toss ribbons with dressing. Yield: 4 servings (serving size: ¾ cup).

Per serving: CALORIES 26 (17% from fat); FAT 0.5g (saturated fat 0.1g); PROTEIN 0.6g; CARBOHYDRATES 4.9g; FIBER 0.7g; CHOLESTEROL 0mg; IRON 0.3mg; SODIUM 378mg; CALCIUM 13mg

Honey Spice Chicken

prep: 7 minutes • **cook:** 11 minutes   *POINTS* value: 5

Chinese five-spice powder can be found in the spice aisle at most supermarkets. Its five assertive spices are cinnamon, cloves, fennel seed, star anise, and Szechwan peppercorns. Substitute fat-free, low-sodium chicken broth for the sherry, if you prefer.

    4 (6-ounce) skinless, boneless chicken breast halves
    ½ teaspoon five-spice powder
    ½ teaspoon salt
    2 teaspoons olive oil
    Cooking spray
    ¼ cup dry sherry
    2 tablespoons honey

1. Place chicken breast halves between 2 sheets of heavy-duty plastic wrap; pound to ¼-inch thickness using a meat mallet or small heavy skillet. Sprinkle both sides of chicken with five-spice powder and salt.

2. Heat olive oil in a large nonstick skillet coated with cooking spray over medium-high heat. Add chicken, and cook 4 to 5 minutes on each side or until done. While chicken cooks, stir together sherry and honey in a small bowl. Remove chicken from pan; keep warm. Add honey mixture to pan; cook, stirring constantly, 2 minutes or until liquid thickens. Return chicken to pan; spoon honey mixture over chicken to glaze. Yield: 4 servings (serving size: 1 chicken breast half).

Per serving: CALORIES 251 (16% from fat); FAT 4.5g (saturated fat 0.9g); PROTEIN 39.4g; CARBOHYDRATES 9.2g; FIBER 0g; CHOLESTEROL 99mg; IRON 1.5mg; SODIUM 403mg; CALCIUM 24mg

Skillet Sesame Asparagus

prep: 1 minute • **cook:** 6 minutes   *POINTS* value: 1

Cut tough ends off 1 pound asparagus, and discard ends. Cut remaining asparagus into 1½-inch pieces. Sauté asparagus in 1 teaspoon dark sesame oil in a large nonstick skillet 2 minutes over medium-high heat. Add 3 tablespoons water to pan; cover and cook 2 minutes. Combine 1 tablespoon low-sodium soy sauce and ¼ teaspoon garlic powder; add to pan, and cook, uncovered, 1 to 2 minutes or until liquid evaporates. Sprinkle ½ teaspoon sesame seeds over asparagus, and cook 30 seconds. Yield: 4 servings (serving size: ½ cup).

Per serving: CALORIES 25 (54% from fat); FAT 1.5g (saturated fat 0.2g); PROTEIN 1.4g; CARBOHYDRATES 2.5g; FIBER 1.1g; CHOLESTEROL 0mg; IRON 1.1mg; SODIUM 233mg; CALCIUM 13mg

Menu

POINTS value: 8

Honey Spice Chicken

Skillet Sesame Asparagus

½ cup whole-grain brown rice
POINTS value: 2

Grocery List

1 pound asparagus spears

1 (5-ounce) bottle dark sesame oil

1 (10-ounce) bottle low-sodium soy sauce

1 (1.25-ounce) jar five-spice powder

1 (2.5-ounce) jar sesame seeds

1 (8.8-ounce) package prepared whole-grain brown rice (such as Uncle Ben's)

1 (750-milliliter) bottle dry sherry

4 (6-ounce) skinless, boneless chicken breast halves

Check staples: olive oil, cooking spray, honey, garlic powder, and salt

pictured on page 124

Lemon-Parsley Chicken

prep: 8 minutes • **cook:** 9 minutes

POINTS value: 5

You can always depend on boneless chicken breasts when you need dinner in a hurry. A simple coating of grated lemon rind and fresh parsley adds bright flavor to this chicken. If you like a bit of tartness, squeeze lemon juice over the chicken just before serving.

- 4 (6-ounce) skinless, boneless chicken breast halves
- ¼ teaspoon salt
- ¼ teaspoon freshly ground black pepper
- ¼ cup finely chopped fresh parsley
- 2 teaspoons grated lemon rind
- 2 teaspoons olive oil
- 1 teaspoon light stick butter

1. Place chicken breast halves between 2 sheets of heavy-duty plastic wrap, and pound to ¼-inch thickness using a meat mallet or small heavy skillet. Sprinkle chicken with salt and pepper.

2. Combine parsley and lemon rind in a small bowl; toss gently. Press half of parsley mixture evenly onto 1 side of chicken.

3. Heat a large nonstick skillet over medium-high heat. Add oil and butter to pan, and heat until butter melts. Add chicken, herb side down, and cook 4 to 5 minutes or until chicken begins to brown. Turn chicken, and top with remaining parsley mixture. Cook 4 to 5 minutes or until done. Yield: 4 servings (serving size: 1 chicken breast half).

Per serving: CALORIES 215 (22% from fat); FAT 5.1g (saturated fat 1.3g); PROTEIN 39.5g; CARBOHYDRATES 0.5g; FIBER 0.3g; CHOLESTEROL 100mg; IRON 1.5mg; SODIUM 263mg; CALCIUM 26mg

Garlic–Pine Nut Couscous

prep: 2 minutes • **cook:** 2 minutes • **other:** 5 minutes

POINTS value: 3

Combine 1 cup water; 1 large garlic clove, crushed; ⅛ teaspoon salt; and ⅛ teaspoon freshly ground black pepper in a medium saucepan. Bring to a boil. Stir in ⅔ cup uncooked plain couscous. Remove from heat, and let stand 5 minutes. Add 2 tablespoons toasted pine nuts, and toss with a fork. Serve immediately. Yield: 4 servings (serving size: about ½ cup).

Per serving: CALORIES 138 (20% from fat); FAT 3.1g (saturated fat 0.2g); PROTEIN 4.3g; CARBOHYDRATES 23.2g; FIBER 1.6g; CHOLESTEROL 0mg; IRON 0.6mg; SODIUM 76mg; CALCIUM 9mg

---

Menu

POINTS value: 8

Lemon-Parsley Chicken

Garlic–Pine Nut Couscous

½ cup steamed asparagus ☑

POINTS value: 0

Grocery List

1 small bunch fresh parsley

2 medium lemons

1 whole garlic head

1 pound asparagus spears

1 (4-ounce) package pine nuts

1 (10-ounce) box uncooked plain couscous

4 (6-ounce) skinless, boneless chicken breast halves

Check staples: light stick butter, olive oil, salt, and black pepper

Tuscan Chicken ☑.

prep: 4 minutes • **cook:** 15 minutes

POINTS value: 5

Simple, rustic dishes made with garden-fresh vegetables characterize Tuscan cuisine. Good-quality olive oil and balsamic vinegar are staple ingredients in most Italian kitchens.

- 4 (6-ounce) skinless, boneless chicken breast halves
- ½ teaspoon salt
- ½ teaspoon dried Italian seasoning
- ¼ teaspoon freshly ground black pepper
- 1 tablespoon olive oil
- 1 pint grape tomatoes
- 2 tablespoons balsamic vinegar
- 1 tablespoon water

1. Place chicken breast halves between 2 sheets of heavy-duty plastic wrap; pound to ½-inch thickness using a meat mallet or small heavy skillet. Sprinkle chicken evenly with salt, Italian seasoning, and pepper.

2. Heat oil in a large nonstick skillet over medium-high heat; add chicken. Cook 3 minutes on each side or until golden. Add tomatoes; cook 4 minutes or until tomato skins pop. Stir in balsamic vinegar and water. Cook 4 minutes or until chicken is done and liquid almost evaporates. Yield: 4 servings (serving size: 1 chicken breast half and about ⅓ cup tomato mixture).

Per serving: CALORIES 238 (22% from fat); FAT 5.8g (saturated fat 1.1g); PROTEIN 40g; CARBOHYDRATES 4.4g; FIBER 0.9g; CHOLESTEROL 99mg; IRON 1.5mg; SODIUM 407mg; CALCIUM 29mg

Grilled Romaine Salad

prep: 4 minutes • **cook:** 5 minutes

POINTS value: 2

Prepare grill. Cut 2 hearts of romaine in half lengthwise. Combine ¼ cup light Northern Italian dressing with basil and Romano (such as Ken's) and 2 crushed garlic cloves; brush cut sides of lettuce with 3 tablespoons dressing mixture. Sprinkle ¼ teaspoon freshly ground black pepper over lettuce. Grill over medium heat 5 minutes or until lettuce is lightly charred. Drizzle an additional ¼ cup dressing evenly over grilled lettuce; top with 2 table-spoons grated fresh Parmesan cheese. Yield: 4 servings (serving size: 1 romaine half).

Per serving: CALORIES 85 (64% from fat); FAT 6g (saturated fat 0.6g); PROTEIN 2.5g; CARBOHYDRATES 5.5g; FIBER 1.3g; CHOLESTEROL 3mg; IRON 1.4mg; SODIUM 386mg; CALCIUM 110mg

Menu

POINTS value: 7

Tuscan Chicken

Grilled Romaine Salad

Grocery List

1 (16-ounce) container grape tomatoes

1 (22-ounce) package hearts of romaine lettuce

1 whole garlic head

1 (8-ounce) bottle light Northern Italian dressing with basil and Romano (such as Ken's)

1 (8-ounce) wedge Parmesan cheese

4 (6-ounce) skinless, boneless chicken breast halves

Check staples: olive oil, balsamic vinegar, dried Italian seasoning, salt, and black pepper

Menu

POINTS value: 5

Cabbage and Apple Chicken

Warm Mustard Potato Salad

Grocery List

1 (10-ounce) package angel hair slaw

1 large Golden Delicious apple

½ pound red potatoes

1 small sweet onion

1 (14-ounce) can fat-free, less-sodium chicken broth

1 (3-ounce) bottle real bacon bits

1 (8-ounce) bottle light olive oil vinaigrette

1 (2.2-ounce) jar caraway seeds

12 (2-ounce) chicken cutlets

Check staples: cooking spray, stone-ground mustard, salt, and black pepper

Cabbage and Apple Chicken ☑.

prep: 4 minutes • **cook:** 15 minutes   *POINTS* value: 4

Preshredded cabbage keeps the preparation time short for this peasant-style dish. Boneless center-cut loin pork chops would make a delicious substitute for the chicken cutlets.

12 (2-ounce) chicken cutlets
 Cooking spray
¼ teaspoon salt
¼ teaspoon freshly ground black pepper
 2 cups packaged angel hair slaw
 1 large Golden Delicious apple, peeled and thinly sliced
½ cup fat-free, less-sodium chicken broth
¼ teaspoon caraway seeds

1. Heat a large nonstick skillet over medium-high heat.

2. Coat chicken with cooking spray, and sprinkle evenly with salt and pepper; add to pan. Cook 2 minutes on each side or until golden brown. Remove chicken, and keep warm.

3. Combine slaw and apple; add to pan, and sauté 5 minutes. Return chicken and accumulated juices to pan. Add broth; bring to a boil, and cook 4 minutes. Add caraway seeds; cook 1 minute. Yield: 4 servings (serving size: 3 chicken cutlets and ½ cup cabbage mixture).

Per serving: CALORIES 223 (8% from fat); FAT 2.1g (saturated fat 0.6g); PROTEIN 40.2g; CARBOHYDRATES 8.9g; FIBER 1.8g; CHOLESTEROL 99mg; IRON 1.4mg; SODIUM 335mg; CALCIUM 22mg

Warm Mustard Potato Salad

prep: 3 minutes • **cook:** 6 minutes   *POINTS* value: 1

Place ½ pound quartered red potatoes and ¼ cup coarsely chopped sweet onion in a small microwave-safe bowl; cover and microwave at HIGH 6 minutes or until tender. Combine 2 tablespoons light olive oil vinaigrette and 1 teaspoon stone-ground mustard in a small bowl; pour over warm potatoes. Toss well, and sprinkle with 1½ teaspoons bottled real bacon bits. Yield: 4 servings (serving size: ½ cup).

Per serving: CALORIES 71 (22% from fat); FAT 1.7g (saturated fat 0.3g); PROTEIN 1.9g; CARBOHYDRATES 12g; FIBER 1g; CHOLESTEROL 1mg; IRON 0.5mg; SODIUM 114mg; CALCIUM 4mg

pictured on page 120

Chicken Thighs with Chipotle-Peach Sauce

prep: 3 minutes • **cook:** 12 minutes   *POINTS* value: 7

Juicy, ripe peaches at their peak season are key to this recipe. If your peaches are firm, let them stand on the kitchen counter for a few days until they're soft to the touch and have an enticing aroma. While the chicken and vegetables grill, you can prepare the chipotle-peach sauce.

1½ pounds skinless, boneless chicken thighs (about 8 thighs)
 ½ teaspoon salt, divided
 ½ teaspoon freshly ground black pepper
    Olive oil–flavored cooking spray
 2 medium peaches, peeled, pitted, and quartered
 2 tablespoons honey
 1 chipotle chile in adobo sauce

1. Prepare grill.
2. Sprinkle chicken with ¼ teaspoon salt and ½ teaspoon pepper; coat with cooking spray. Place chicken on grill rack coated with cooking spray. Grill 12 minutes or until done, turning chicken once.
3. While chicken cooks, puree peaches, honey, chile, and remaining ¼ teaspoon salt in a food processor. Reserve ¾ cup chipotle-peach sauce to serve with chicken; brush remaining ½ cup sauce over chicken during last 2 minutes of cooking. Yield: 4 servings (serving size: about 2 thighs and 3 tablespoons sauce).

Per serving: CALORIES 299 (39% from fat); FAT 12.9g (saturated fat 3.6g); PROTEIN 31g; CARBOHYDRATES 13.9g; FIBER 1.1g; CHOLESTEROL 112mg; IRON 1.8mg; SODIUM 428mg; CALCIUM 19mg

Grilled Corn and Red Pepper Salad ☑.

prep: 7 minutes • **cook:** 12 minutes   *POINTS* value: 1

Prepare grill. Coat 2 ears shucked corn and 2 halved and seeded red bell peppers with olive oil–flavored cooking spray. Place on grill rack coated with cooking spray. Grill 6 minutes on each side or until slightly charred. Cut corn from cob; cut bell pepper into strips. Place in a bowl with 2 chopped green onions, 2 tablespoons fresh lime juice, ¼ teaspoon salt, and ¼ teaspoon freshly ground black pepper. Toss well. Yield: 4 servings (serving size: about ⅔ cup).

Per serving: CALORIES 95 (16% from fat); FAT 1.7g (saturated fat 0.5g); PROTEIN 3.3g; CARBOHYDRATES 17.9g; FIBER 5g; CHOLESTEROL 0mg; IRON 0.9mg; SODIUM 154mg; CALCIUM 41mg

Menu

POINTS value: 8

Chicken Thighs with Chipotle-Peach Sauce

Grilled Corn and Red Pepper Salad

Grocery List

2 medium peaches

2 medium ears shucked corn

2 medium red bell peppers

1 small bunch green onions

1 small lime

1 (7.5-ounce) can chipotle chiles in adobo sauce

1½ pounds skinless, boneless chicken thighs (about 8 thighs)

Check staples: olive oil–flavored cooking spray, honey, salt, and black pepper

Menu

POINTS value: 9

Chicken Succotash

Grocery List

1 small red bell pepper

1 small onion

1 (10-ounce) package frozen whole-kernel corn

1 (10-ounce) package frozen baby lima beans

1 (3-pound) whole chicken

Check staples: salt and black pepper

Chicken Succotash

prep: 7 minutes • **cook:** 3 hours, 30 minutes   *POINTS* value: 9

You'll be welcomed home by the pleasant smell of this classic Southern favorite gently simmering in your slow cooker. This dish is a complete meal, but for heartier fare and an additional *POINTS* value of 2, serve it over ½ cup of brown or white rice.

    1   (10-ounce) package frozen whole-kernel corn
    1   (10-ounce) package frozen baby lima beans
    1   small red bell pepper, diced
    1   small onion, diced
    ¼   cup water
    ¾   teaspoon salt, divided
    ½   teaspoon freshly ground black pepper, divided
    1   (3-pound) whole chicken

1. Combine first 5 ingredients, ¼ teaspoon salt, and ¼ teaspoon black pepper in the bottom of a 5-quart electric slow cooker.

2. Remove and discard giblets and neck from chicken. Trim excess fat. Sprinkle chicken with remaining ½ teaspoon salt and ¼ teaspoon pepper. Place chicken on top of vegetables in slow cooker.

3. Cover and cook on HIGH 3½ hours or until chicken is done. Remove skin from chicken; discard. Yield: 4 servings (serving size: 1 chicken quarter and 1¼ cups vegetables).

Per serving: CALORIES 431 (24% from fat); FAT 11.5g (saturated fat 2.8g); PROTEIN 43.2g; CARBOHYDRATES 35.5g; FIBER 6.7g; CHOLESTEROL 138mg; IRON 7.2mg; SODIUM 630mg; CALCIUM 55mg

Easy Turkey Lasagna

prep: 7 minutes • **cook:** 54 minutes • **other:** 10 minutes   *POINTS* value: 6

While the total cook time for this hearty lasagna is about 1 hour, it takes only a few minutes to get it ready to go in the oven. Precooked lasagna noodles absorb the liquid from the tomato sauce during baking, eliminating the need to preboil them.

1½   pounds ground turkey breast
1   (26-ounce) jar tomato-basil pasta sauce (such as Classico)
Cooking spray
9   precooked lasagna noodles
1   (16-ounce) carton 1% low-fat cottage cheese
2   cups (8 ounces) shredded part-skim mozzarella cheese
¼   cup hot water

1. Preheat oven to 350°.
2. Heat a large nonstick skillet over medium-high heat; add turkey. Cook 9 minutes or until turkey is cooked, stirring to crumble. Add sauce; bring to a boil. Remove from heat.
3. Coat a 13 x 9–inch baking dish with cooking spray; spread 1 cup turkey mixture in bottom of dish. Arrange 3 noodles over turkey mixture; top with half of cottage cheese, 1 cup turkey mixture, and ⅔ cup mozzarella cheese. Repeat layers once, placing last 3 noodles directly on cheese and topping with remaining 2 cups turkey mixture and ⅔ cup mozzarella cheese. Pour water around inside edge of dish onto edges of noodles. Cover and bake at 350° for 30 minutes. Uncover and bake 15 minutes or until cheese melts and begins to brown. Let stand 10 minutes. Cut into 10 equal portions. Yield: 10 servings (serving size: 1 [4½ x 2⅔–inch] rectangle).

Per serving: CALORIES 277 (32% from fat); FAT 9.9g (saturated fat 4.2g); PROTEIN 27.1g; CARBOHYDRATES 20.5g; FIBER 1.8g; CHOLESTEROL 59mg; IRON 1.1mg; SODIUM 539mg; CALCIUM 291mg

Greek Vegetable Salad

prep: 15 minutes   *POINTS* value: 1

Combine 8 cups torn romaine lettuce, 4 cups halved grape tomatoes, 2 cups sliced cucumber, ½ cup crumbled feta cheese, and 16 pitted kalamata olives in a large bowl. Add ½ cup fat-free red wine vinaigrette; toss to coat. Yield: 10 servings (serving size: 1 cup).

Per serving: CALORIES 74 (43% from fat); FAT 3.5g (saturated fat 1.4g); PROTEIN 2.4g; CARBOHYDRATES 9.3g; FIBER 1.9g; CHOLESTEROL 7mg; IRON 0.7mg; SODIUM 308mg; CALCIUM 63mg

Menu

POINTS value: 7

Easy Turkey Lasagna

Greek Vegetable Salad

Grocery List

1 (10-ounce) package torn romaine lettuce

2 (16-ounce) containers grape tomatoes

1 large cucumber

1 (26-ounce) jar tomato-basil pasta sauce (such as Classico)

1 (8-ounce) bottle fat-free red wine vinaigrette

1 (7-ounce) jar pitted kalamata olives

1 (8-ounce) package precooked lasagna noodles

1 (16-ounce) carton 1% low-fat cottage cheese

1 (8-ounce) package shredded part-skim mozzarella cheese

1 (6-ounce) container crumbled feta cheese

1½ pounds ground turkey breast

Check staples: cooking spray

Menu

POINTS value: 8

Turkey Picadillo

Bell Pepper Sauté

1 (6-inch) flour tortilla
POINTS value: 2

Grocery List

1 small bunch green onions

1 large yellow bell pepper

1 large green bell pepper

1 large shallot

1 small bunch fresh parsley

1 (11.3-ounce) package (6-inch) flour tortillas

1 (9-ounce) box raisins

1 (4-ounce) package pine nuts (optional)

1 (15-ounce) can seasoned diced tomato sauce for chili (such as Hunt's)

1¼ pounds ground turkey breast

Check staples: olive oil, cider vinegar, ground cumin, salt, and black pepper

Turkey Picadillo

prep: 1 minute • **cook:** 14 minutes
POINTS value: 5

We substituted lean ground turkey meat for ground beef in this flavorful Cuban dish. To serve, wrap it in a warm flour tortilla or spoon it over brown rice. Many grocery stores carry multipacks of green, red, and yellow bell peppers that are often less expensive than purchasing each pepper individually.

1¼   pounds ground turkey breast
  2   teaspoons ground cumin
  1   (15-ounce) can seasoned diced tomato sauce for chili (such as Hunt's)
¼   cup water
½   cup raisins
  1   tablespoon cider vinegar
¼   teaspoon black pepper
¼   cup sliced green onions
Toasted pine nuts (optional)

1. Heat a large nonstick skillet over medium-high heat; add turkey and cumin. Cook 7 minutes or until turkey is browned, stirring to crumble. Stir in tomato sauce and next 4 ingredients; bring to a boil. Cover, reduce heat, and simmer 5 minutes. Sprinkle with green onions before serving, and top with pine nuts, if desired. Yield: 4 servings (serving size: about 1 cup).

Per serving: CALORIES 263 (7% from fat); FAT 2.2g (saturated fat 0g); PROTEIN 37.6g; CARBOHYDRATES 25.9g; FIBER 3.1g; CHOLESTEROL 56mg; IRON 2.7mg; SODIUM 877mg; CALCIUM 24mg

Bell Pepper Sauté ✓

prep: 3 minutes • **cook:** 7 minutes
POINTS value: 1

Heat 2 teaspoons olive oil in a large nonstick skillet over medium-high heat. Cut 1 large yellow bell pepper and 1 large green bell pepper into julienne strips. Chop 1 large shallot. Add bell pepper strips and shallot to pan; sprinkle vegetables with ⅛ teaspoon salt. Cook 5 minutes or until bell peppers are crisp-tender. Stir in 1 tablespoon parsley and ¼ teaspoon black pepper; cook 1 minute. Yield: 4 servings (serving size: ¾ cup).

Per serving: CALORIES 59 (38% from fat); FAT 2.5g (saturated fat 0.4g); PROTEIN 1.8g; CARBOHYDRATES 9.3g; FIBER 1.6g; CHOLESTEROL 0mg; IRON 0.7mg; SODIUM 76mg; CALCIUM 9mg

Turkey Cutlets with Cranberry-Cherry Sauce

prep: 2 minutes • **cook:** 13 minutes
POINTS value: 6

Turkey and cranberries are simply meant for each other. Our simplified version of the traditional holiday combination is perfect for any hectic weeknight. Turkey cutlets cook quickly; watch them carefully so that they don't overcook.

1½	pounds turkey cutlets
½	teaspoon salt
½	teaspoon freshly ground black pepper
1	tablespoon olive oil, divided
½	(12-ounce) container cranberry-orange crushed fruit
¼	cup dried cherries
1½	teaspoons balsamic vinegar
½	teaspoon grated peeled fresh ginger

1. Sprinkle turkey evenly with salt and pepper.
2. Heat 1½ teaspoons oil in a large nonstick skillet over medium-high heat. Add half of turkey, and cook 2 minutes on each side or until done. Remove turkey; keep warm. Repeat with remaining turkey and oil.
3. Add cranberry-orange crushed fruit and next 3 ingredients to pan. Bring mixture to a boil over medium-high heat. Return turkey to pan, and nestle in cranberry-cherry sauce. Cover, reduce heat to medium-low, and simmer 3 minutes or until turkey is thoroughly heated. Remove cutlets from pan, and serve with cranberry-cherry sauce. Yield: 4 servings (serving size: about 2 cutlets and 3 tablespoons sauce).

Per serving: CALORIES 321 (12% from fat); FAT 4.3g (saturated fat 0.5g); PROTEIN 42.3g; CARBOHYDRATES 25.9g; FIBER 1.7g; CHOLESTEROL 68mg; IRON 2.4mg; SODIUM 449mg; CALCIUM 11mg

Roasted Brussels Sprouts

prep: 6 minutes • **cook:** 15 minutes
POINTS value: 1

Preheat oven to 450°. Combine 1 teaspoon grated orange rind, 1 tablespoon fresh orange juice, and 2 teaspoons olive oil in a small bowl. Place 1 pound halved Brussels sprouts on a jelly-roll pan coated with cooking spray; drizzle orange juice mixture over sprouts, and toss until coated. Sprinkle evenly with ½ teaspoon salt and ¼ teaspoon freshly ground black pepper. Bake at 450° for 15 to 20 minutes or until edges of sprouts look lightly browned and crisp. Yield: 4 servings (serving size: about ¾ cup).

Per serving: CALORIES 71 (29% from fat); FAT 2.7g (saturated fat 0.4g); PROTEIN 3.9g; CARBOHYDRATES 10.8g; FIBER 4.4g; CHOLESTEROL 0mg; IRON 1.6mg; SODIUM 319mg; CALCIUM 50mg

Menu

POINTS value: 7

Turkey Cutlets with Cranberry-Cherry Sauce

Roasted Brussels Sprouts

Grocery List

1 small piece ginger

1 small orange

1 pound Brussels sprouts

1 (5-ounce) package dried cherries

1 (12-ounce) container cranberry-orange crushed fruit

1½ pounds turkey cutlets

Check staples: olive oil, cooking spray, balsamic vinegar, salt, and black pepper

Menu

POINTS value: 5

Polenta with Italian-Sausage Red Sauce

Spinach and Mushroom Salad

Grocery List

2 (8-ounce) packages presliced mushrooms

1 small bunch fresh basil (optional)

1 (16-ounce) container grape tomatoes

1 (5- or 6-ounce) package baby spinach

1 small red onion

1 (16-ounce) tube of polenta

1 (26-ounce) jar tomato-basil pasta sauce (such as Classico)

1 (8-ounce) bottle fat-free balsamic vinaigrette

4 ounces mild turkey Italian sausage

Check staples: cooking spray

Polenta with Italian-Sausage Red Sauce

prep: 3 minutes • **cook:** 12 minutes   *POINTS* value: 5

These polenta rounds offer a tasty change of pace from traditional spaghetti and meat sauce. Look for polenta in the produce section at your supermarket.

- 4   ounces mild turkey Italian sausage
- 1   (8-ounce) package presliced mushrooms
- 1   (16-ounce) tube of polenta
- Cooking spray
- 2   cups tomato-basil pasta sauce (such as Classico)
- Chopped fresh basil (optional)

1. Remove casings from sausage. Heat a large nonstick skillet over medium-high heat; add sausage and mushrooms. Cook 7 minutes or until sausage is browned, stirring to crumble.

2. While sausage and mushrooms cook, cut polenta crosswise into 12 slices. Pat both sides dry with paper towels; coat slices with cooking spray. Heat a large nonstick skillet over medium-high heat. Coat pan with cooking spray. Add polenta slices, and cook 6 minutes on each side or until browned.

3. While polenta cooks, add pasta sauce to sausage mixture; simmer 5 minutes or until thoroughly heated. Serve over polenta. Sprinkle with chopped fresh basil, if desired. Yield: 6 servings (serving size: 2 slices polenta and ½ cup sauce).

Per serving: CALORIES 295 (12% from fat); FAT 3.8g (saturated fat 0g); PROTEIN 10.9g; CARBOHYDRATES 53.5g; FIBER 5.1g; CHOLESTEROL 11mg; IRON 2.1mg; SODIUM 437mg; CALCIUM 68mg

Spinach and Mushroom Salad ☑.

prep: 4 minutes   *POINTS* value: 0

Combine 2 cups halved grape tomatoes, 4 cups fresh baby spinach, 1 (8-ounce) package presliced mushrooms, and ¼ cup thinly sliced red onion in a large bowl. Pour ¼ cup fat-free balsamic vinaigrette over salad; toss gently to coat. Yield: 6 servings (serving size: about 1 cup).

Per serving: CALORIES 32 (6% from fat); FAT 0.2g (saturated fat 0g); PROTEIN 2.1g; CARBOHYDRATES 6.5g; FIBER 1.9g; CHOLESTEROL 0mg; IRON 0.9mg; SODIUM 167mg; CALCIUM 19mg

Salads

Menu

POINTS value: 8

Citrus, Salmon, and Fennel Salad

Orange Drop Biscuits

Grocery List

1 medium lime

2 (6.5-ounce) packages sweet butter lettuce blend

1 large fennel bulb

2 medium navel oranges

1 (14-ounce) bottle light olive oil vinaigrette

1 (2-pound) box low-fat baking mix (such as Bisquick)

2 (6.3-ounce) packages frozen grilled salmon fillets (such as Gorton's)

Check staples: 1% low-fat milk, cooking spray, and powdered sugar

Citrus, Salmon, and Fennel Salad

prep: 9 minutes • **cook:** 7 minutes   *POINTS* value: 4

The mild acidity of the fresh oranges cuts the richness of the salmon and adds bright flavor to this dish. Assemble the salad while the biscuits bake.

  2 (6.3-ounce) packages frozen grilled salmon fillets (such as Gorton's)
  2 (6.5-ounce) packages sweet butter lettuce blend
  1 large fennel bulb, thinly sliced
  1 navel orange
  ⅓ cup light olive oil vinaigrette
  1 tablespoon fresh lime juice

1. Cook salmon fillets in the microwave according to package directions. Break fish into large chunks with a fork. Chill while preparing salad.

2. Combine lettuce and fennel in a large bowl. Peel and section orange; set sections aside. Squeeze remaining membranes over a small bowl to extract juice; discard membranes. Top lettuce with orange sections. Combine vinaigrette and lime juice with orange juice, stirring with a whisk. Add fish to lettuce mixture, and drizzle with vinaigrette mixture. Toss gently to combine. Yield: 4 servings (serving size: about 3 cups).

Per serving: CALORIES 177 (37% from fat); FAT 7.3g (saturated fat 0.9g); PROTEIN 17.9g; CARBOHYDRATES 11.4g; FIBER 2.5g; CHOLESTEROL 35mg; IRON 1.7mg; SODIUM 447mg; CALCIUM 58mg

Orange Drop Biscuits

prep: 3 minutes • **cook:** 9 minutes   *POINTS* value: 4

Preheat oven to 450°. Combine 1 cup low-fat baking mix (such as Bisquick) and ⅓ cup 1% low-fat milk, stirring just until moist. Drop dough onto a baking sheet coated with cooking spray; coat dough with cooking spray. Bake at 450° for 9 minutes or until biscuits are lightly browned. Meanwhile, combine ½ cup powdered sugar, 1 teaspoon grated orange rind, and 2 teaspoons fresh orange juice. Drizzle orange glaze over warm biscuits. Serve immediately. Yield: 4 servings (serving size: 1 biscuit).

Per serving: CALORIES 175 (11% from fat); FAT 2.1g (saturated fat 0.1g); PROTEIN 3g; CARBOHYDRATES 36.8g; FIBER 0.4g; CHOLESTEROL 1mg; IRON 1.1mg; SODIUM 336mg; CALCIUM 140mg

Lemon-Pepper Tuna Pasta Salad

prep: 4 minutes • **cook:** 14 minutes   *POINTS* value: 6

Use packages of lemon and cracked pepper–flavored tuna to jump-start this pasta salad.

2½   cups multigrain penne (such as Barilla Plus)
  3   (4-ounce) packages lemon and cracked pepper–flavored albacore tuna steak, drained
  ½   cup thinly sliced red onion
  ¼   cup chopped fresh flat-leaf parsley
  2   teaspoons olive oil
  ½   teaspoon salt
  ½   teaspoon freshly ground black pepper

1. Cook pasta according to package directions, omitting salt and fat. Drain, reserving 2 tablespoons pasta water.
2. Combine pasta, reserved pasta water, fish, and remaining ingredients in a large bowl; stir well. Serve immediately. Yield: 4 servings (serving size: about 2 cups).

Per serving: CALORIES 345 (11% from fat); FAT 4.1g (saturated fat 0.3g); PROTEIN 37.2g; CARBOHYDRATES 39g; FIBER 4.4g; CHOLESTEROL 38mg; IRON 2.1mg; SODIUM 596mg; CALCIUM 29mg

Parmesan Peas

prep: 6 minutes   *POINTS* value: 1

Place 2 cups frozen petite peas in a colander, and rinse under cool water until thawed; drain well. Combine 1 tablespoon grated fresh Parmesan cheese, 2 teaspoons grated fresh lemon rind, and 1 teaspoon fresh lemon juice with peas in a medium bowl; toss well to coat. Yield: 4 servings (serving size: ½ cup).

Per serving: CALORIES 64 (9% from fat); FAT 0.8g (saturated fat 0.3g); PROTEIN 4.5g; CARBOHYDRATES 10.1g; FIBER 3.1g; CHOLESTEROL 1mg; IRON 1.1mg; SODIUM 112mg; CALCIUM 42mg

Menu

POINTS value: 7

Lemon-Pepper Tuna Pasta Salad

Parmesan Peas

Grocery List

1 small red onion

1 small bunch fresh flat-leaf parsley

1 small lemon

3 (4-ounce) packages lemon and cracked pepper–flavored albacore tuna steak

1 (14.5-ounce) package multi-grain penne (such as Barilla Plus)

1 (8-ounce) wedge Parmesan cheese

1 (16-ounce) package frozen petite green peas

Check staples: olive oil, salt, and black pepper

Grilled Shrimp Salad

9 thin breadsticks
POINTS value: 3

Grocery List

2 (7-ounce) bags veggie spring mix salad (such as Fresh Express)

1 (2-ounce) bag slivered almonds

1 (16-ounce) bottle light sesame ginger dressing

1 (3-ounce) package thin breadsticks

1½ pounds peeled and deveined large shrimp

Check staples: cooking spray

Grilled Shrimp Salad

prep: 2 minutes • **cook:** 6 minutes • **other:** 5 minutes   *POINTS* value: 6

A store-bought sesame ginger dressing helps keep the number of ingredients short for this menu while providing richness.

1½ pounds peeled and deveined large shrimp
 ½ cup plus 2 tablespoons light sesame ginger dressing, divided
  Cooking spray
  2 (7-ounce) bags veggie spring mix salad (such as Fresh Express)
 ¼ cup slivered almonds, toasted

1. Preheat grill.
2. Combine shrimp and ¼ cup dressing in a large bowl; toss to coat. Let stand 5 minutes.
3. Thread shrimp evenly onto 8 (8-inch) skewers. Place skewers on grill rack coated with cooking spray, and grill 3 minutes on each side or until done. Remove shrimp from skewers.
4. Arrange greens on plates; top evenly with shrimp and almonds. Drizzle evenly with remaining dressing. Yield: 4 servings (serving size: 2¼ cups greens, 4 ounces shrimp, 1 tablespoon almonds, and 1½ tablespoons dressing).

Per serving: CALORIES 267 (34% from fat); FAT 10.2g (saturated fat 2.5g); PROTEIN 31.9g; CARBOHYDRATES 11.4g; FIBER 2.4g; CHOLESTEROL 262mg; IRON 4.9mg; SODIUM 850mg; CALCIUM 162mg

pictured on page 114

Shrimp, Avocado, and Corn Salad

prep: 10 minutes   *POINTS* value: 5

Buy cooked shrimp from your local seafood market or try using frozen cooked shrimp—just quick-thaw it under cold running water.

- 1   pound cooked peeled medium shrimp
- 1   cup frozen whole-kernel corn, thawed
- 1   cup fresh cilantro leaves
- 1   (10-ounce) package torn romaine lettuce
- ⅓ cup light lime vinaigrette
- ½ teaspoon freshly ground black pepper
- 1   medium avocado, peeled and diced

1. Combine first 6 ingredients in a large bowl. Add avocado; toss gently. Yield: 4 servings (serving size: 2¼ cups).

Per serving: CALORIES 259 (35% from fat); FAT 10g (saturated fat 1.4g); PROTEIN 27.3g; CARBOHYDRATES 17.4g; FIBER 4.1g; CHOLESTEROL 221mg; IRON 5mg; SODIUM 577mg; CALCIUM 73mg

Jalapeño-Cilantro Tortilla Chips

prep: 2 minutes • **cook:** 9 minutes   *POINTS* value: 1

Preheat oven to 425°. Lightly coat 2 (8½-inch) jalapeño-cilantro flour tortillas on both sides with cooking spray; cut each tortilla into 8 wedges. Place wedges on a baking sheet; sprinkle with ⅛ teaspoon salt. Bake at 425° for 9 minutes or until crisp, turning once. Yield: 4 servings (serving size: 4 wedges).

Per serving: CALORIES 60 (15% from fat); FAT 1g (saturated fat 0.3g); PROTEIN 2g; CARBOHYDRATES 11.5g; FIBER 0.5g; CHOLESTEROL 0mg; IRON 1.4mg; SODIUM 125mg; CALCIUM 50mg

Menu

POINTS value: 6

Shrimp, Avocado, and Corn Salad

Jalapeño-Cilantro Tortilla Chips

Grocery List

1 medium avocado

1 small bunch fresh cilantro

1 (10-ounce) package torn romaine lettuce

1 (12.7-ounce) package (8½-inch) jalapeño-cilantro flour tortillas

1 (16-ounce) bottle light lime vinaigrette

1 (10-ounce) package frozen whole-kernel corn

1 pound cooked peeled medium shrimp

Check staples: cooking spray, salt, and black pepper

Menu

POINTS value: 8

**Mediterranean
Pasta Salad**

1 cup cubed cantaloupe ☑.
POINTS value: 1

Grocery List

¼ pound asparagus spears

1 (16-ounce) container grape
tomatoes

1 small bunch fresh basil

1 (32-ounce) container cubed
cantaloupe

2 thin slices prosciutto (about
1 ounce)

1 (14-ounce) can quartered
artichoke hearts

1 (7-ounce) jar pitted kalamata
olives

1 (12-ounce) bottle roasted red
bell peppers

1 (16-ounce) jar light balsamic
vinaigrette

1 (8-ounce) package Monterey
Jack cheese with jalapeño
peppers

1 (9-ounce) package refrigerated
three-cheese tortellini

Mediterranean Pasta Salad

prep: 5 minutes • **cook:** 10 minutes   *POINTS* value: 7

**Look for containers of fresh cubed cantaloupe in the produce section of the super-
market or at the salad bar. Freeze leftover tortellini in a zip-top plastic bag to use
later in a soup or side dish.**

½ (9-ounce) package refrigerated three-cheese tortellini
¼ pound asparagus spears, trimmed
⅓ cup bottled roasted red bell peppers, cut into 1-inch pieces
1 ounce Monterey Jack cheese with jalapeño peppers, cut into ¼-inch cubes
    (about ¼ cup)
6 drained canned quartered artichoke hearts
8 grape tomatoes
8 pitted kalamata olives
2 thin slices prosciutto, cut crosswise into strips (about 1 ounce)
1 tablespoon chopped fresh basil
3 tablespoons light balsamic vinaigrette

1. Cook pasta in 1 quart boiling water 6 minutes, omitting salt and fat. Add asparagus
to boiling water, and cook 1 minute. Drain in a colander, and rinse with cold water until
cooled. Drain.

2. While pasta cooks, combine roasted bell peppers and next 7 ingredients in a large bowl.
Add tortellini and asparagus; toss gently. Yield: 3 servings (serving size: 1⅓ cups).

Per serving: CALORIES 304 (47% from fat); FAT 16.2g (saturated fat 4.7g); PROTEIN 11.2g; CARBOHYDRATES 29.7g; FIBER 2.2g;
CHOLESTEROL 28mg; IRON 0.6mg; SODIUM 876mg; CALCIUM 82mg

pictured on page 42

Pea, Carrot, and Tofu Salad

prep: 3 minutes • **cook:** 10 minutes   *POINTS* value: 7

This lively salad is chock-full of colorful veggies and delightful crunch. Drain the tofu slices between several layers of paper towels to absorb the extra moisture so the tofu will brown quickly.

1   (14-ounce) package water-packed firm tofu, drained
2   tablespoons sesame oil
½   cup light sesame ginger dressing
1   (16-ounce) package frozen petite green peas, thawed
1   cup matchstick-cut carrots
1   (8-ounce) can water chestnuts, drained
½   cup thinly sliced red onion
¼   teaspoon freshly ground black pepper
1   medium head Bibb lettuce, torn
4   teaspoons roasted, unsalted sunflower seed kernels

1. Place tofu on several layers of heavy-duty paper towels. Cover tofu with additional paper towels; gently press out moisture. Cut tofu into 1-inch cubes.
2. Heat oil in a large nonstick skillet over medium-high heat. Add tofu; cook 5 to 6 minutes on each side or until golden on all sides, stirring occasionally.
3. Combine tofu, dressing, and next 5 ingredients in a large bowl. Toss gently to coat. Divide lettuce evenly among 4 plates. Top lettuce with 1¾ cups tofu mixture. Sprinkle evenly with sunflower seed kernels. Yield: 4 servings (serving size: about 1½ cups lettuce, 1¾ cups tofu mixture, and 1 teaspoon sunflower seed kernels).

Per serving: CALORIES 312 (40% from fat); FAT 14.6g (saturated fat 2.1g); PROTEIN 15.9g; CARBOHYDRATES 33.2g; FIBER 8.5g; CHOLESTEROL 0mg; IRON 4.4mg; SODIUM 554mg; CALCIUM 256mg

Menu

POINTS value: 8

Pea, Carrot, and Tofu Salad

2 sesame crispbreads
POINTS value: 1

Grocery List

1 small red onion

1 (10-ounce) package matchstick-cut carrots

1 medium head Bibb lettuce

1 (14-ounce) package water-packed firm tofu

1 (7.25-ounce) package roasted, unsalted sunflower seed kernels

1 (8-ounce) can water chestnuts

1 (5-ounce) bottle sesame oil

1 (14-ounce) bottle light sesame ginger dressing

1 (7-ounce) box sesame crispbreads (such as Wasa)

1 (16-ounce) package frozen petite green peas, thawed

Check staples: black pepper

pictured on page 36

Arugula Salad with Prosciutto and Pears

prep: 7 minutes • **cook:** 2 minutes   *POINTS* value: 6

You can toast the walnuts quickly in a dry skillet over medium-high heat. Stir frequently and remove them from the heat as soon as you begin to smell that wonderful nutty aroma.

- 2 (5-ounce) bags arugula
- 2 red pears, cored and cut lengthwise into ¼-inch-thick slices
- 4 thin slices prosciutto, cut crosswise into strips (about 2 ounces)
- ¾ cup shaved fresh Parmesan cheese (about 3 ounces)
- 4 tablespoons walnut halves, toasted
- 3 tablespoons white wine vinegar
- 2 tablespoons olive oil
- ¼ teaspoon salt
- ⅛ teaspoon pepper

1. Combine first 5 ingredients in a large bowl.

2. Combine vinegar and next 3 ingredients in a small bowl, stirring with a whisk. Drizzle over salad; toss gently to coat. Yield: 4 servings (serving size: about 2¾ cups).

Per serving: CALORIES 251 (68% from fat); FAT 19.1g (saturated fat 5.4g); PROTEIN 13.2g; CARBOHYDRATES 10.1g; FIBER 3.3g; CHOLESTEROL 27mg; IRON 1mg; SODIUM 713mg; CALCIUM 301mg

French Bread with Herbed Goat Cheese Spread

prep: 6 minutes • **cook:** 1 minute   *POINTS* value: 3

Combine 2 ounces softened goat cheese, ½ teaspoon chopped fresh oregano, ½ teaspoon chopped fresh thyme, and ¼ teaspoon freshly ground black pepper. Spread evenly on 8 toasted ½-inch-thick diagonally cut slices whole wheat baguette. Yield: 4 servings (serving size: 2 slices).

Per serving: CALORIES 134 (32% from fat); FAT 4.8g (saturated fat 3.1g); PROTEIN 6.4g; CARBOHYDRATES 16.4g; FIBER 0.7g; CHOLESTEROL 11mg; IRON 1.3mg; SODIUM 257mg; CALCIUM 55mg

Menu

POINTS value: 9

Arugula Salad with Prosciutto and Pears

French Bread with Herbed Goat Cheese Spread

Grocery List

2 (5-ounce) bags arugula

2 red pears

1 small bunch fresh oregano

1 small bunch fresh thyme

1 (8.5-ounce) thin whole wheat baguette

4 thin slices prosciutto (about 2 ounces)

1 (4-ounce) package walnut halves

1 (8-ounce) wedge Parmesan cheese

1 (3-ounce) package goat cheese

Check staples: olive oil, white wine vinegar, salt, and black pepper

Orecchiette and Roasted Chicken Salad

prep: 5 minutes • **cook:** 14 minutes   *POINTS* value: 5

A small amount of a good-quality blue cheese adds superior taste to this pasta salad. We recommend using Maytag cheese because of its mild flavor, but if you prefer a stronger-flavored cheese, you can substitute Stilton or Gorgonzola.

2½ cups uncooked orecchiette ("little ears" pasta)
 4 cups chopped spinach
 2 cups chopped roasted chicken breast
 ⅓ cup light blue cheese dressing (such as Marie's)
 ½ cup (2 ounces) crumbled Maytag blue cheese
 ½ cup coarsely chopped walnuts, toasted (optional)

1. Cook pasta according to package directions, omitting salt and fat. While pasta cooks, combine spinach, chicken, and dressing in a large bowl. Toss with cooked pasta; top with crumbled blue cheese and, if desired, chopped walnuts. Yield: 6 servings (serving size: 1 cup salad and about 1 tablespoon blue cheese).

Per serving: CALORIES 265 (18% from fat); FAT 5.4g (saturated fat 2.5g); PROTEIN 22.5g; CARBOHYDRATES 31g; FIBER 1.6g; CHOLESTEROL 48mg; IRON 2.3mg; SODIUM 413mg; CALCIUM 93mg

Menu

POINTS value: 6

Orecchiette and Roasted Chicken Salad

1 cup fresh strawberry, melon, and grape mix ✔.
  POINTS value: 1

Grocery List

1 (5- or 6-ounce) package fresh spinach

1 (12-ounce) jar light blue cheese dressing (such as Marie's)

1 (64-ounce) container fresh strawberry, melon, and grape mix

1 (2-pound) rotisserie chicken

1 (4-ounce) package chopped walnuts (optional)

1 (16-ounce) package orecchiette ("little ears" pasta)

1 (4-ounce) package Maytag blue cheese

pictured on page 46

Couscous Salad with Roasted Chicken

prep: 8 minutes • **cook:** 2 minutes • **other:** 5 minutes   *POINTS* value: 5

This hearty chicken salad is full of fragrant herbs and vegetables. For an extra kick of flavor and an additional *POINTS* value of 1, sprinkle the salad with 1 tablespoon feta cheese.

  ⅓ cup uncooked couscous
1½ cups chopped roasted chicken breast
  1 cup chopped English cucumber
  1 cup halved grape tomatoes
  1 cup chopped fresh parsley
  ¼ cup chopped fresh mint
  4 green onions, chopped
  1 garlic clove, minced
  ¼ cup fresh lemon juice
  2 tablespoons olive oil
  ¼ teaspoon salt

1. Prepare couscous according to package directions, omitting salt and fat. Fluff couscous with a fork.

2. Combine couscous, chicken, and next 6 ingredients in a large bowl. Set aside.

3. Combine lemon juice, olive oil, and salt in a small bowl; stir well with a whisk. Pour dressing over couscous mixture. Yield: 4 servings (serving size: about 1 cup).

Per serving: CALORIES 230 (37% from fat); FAT 9.3g (saturated fat 1.6g); PROTEIN 19.7g; CARBOHYDRATES 17.7g; FIBER 2.8g; CHOLESTEROL 45mg; IRON 2.7mg; SODIUM 356mg; CALCIUM 66mg

Grocery List

1 small English cucumber

1 (16-ounce) container grape tomatoes

1 small bunch fresh parsley

1 small bunch fresh mint

1 small bunch green onions

1 whole garlic head

2 medium lemons

1 (12-ounce) package (6-inch) pitas

1 (2-pound) rotisserie chicken

1 (10-ounce) box uncooked couscous

Check staples: olive oil, olive oil–flavored cooking spray, salt-free Greek seasoning, and salt

Greek Pita Chips

prep: 6 minutes • **cook:** 15 minutes   *POINTS* value: 2

Preheat oven to 350°. Split 2 (6-inch) pitas into 2 rounds each. Cut each round into 8 wedges. Place wedges on a lightly greased baking sheet. Coat rough side of each wedge with olive oil–flavored cooking spray. Sprinkle evenly with ¼ teaspoon salt-free Greek seasoning and ¼ teaspoon salt. Bake at 350° for 15 minutes or until crisp. Yield: 4 servings (serving size: 8 chips).

Per serving: CALORIES 82 (2% from fat); FAT 0.2g (saturated fat 0g); PROTEIN 3.5g; CARBOHYDRATES 16.5g; FIBER 0.5g; CHOLESTEROL 0mg; IRON 1.4mg; SODIUM 225mg; CALCIUM 20mg

Sandwiches

Menu

POINTS value: 10

Open-Faced Salmon BLTs

Tomato and Cucumber
Salad

Grocery List

1 medium lemon

1 small bunch fresh dill

1 small head green leaf lettuce

1 small tomato

1 (16-ounce) container cherry
tomatoes

2 small salad cucumbers

1 small yellow or green bell
pepper

1 (12-ounce) loaf French bread

1 (16-ounce) bottle light red
wine vinaigrette

1 (2.2-ounce) package precooked
hickory-smoked bacon (such as
Jimmy Dean)

2 (6-ounce) salmon fillets (about
1 inch thick)

Check staples: light mayonnaise, cooking spray, and black

Open-Faced Salmon BLTs

prep: 5 minutes • **cook:** 10 minutes   *POINTS* value: 8

Fresh salmon and a tangy dill spread dress up the traditional BLT. You'll need a knife and fork to handle this hearty sandwich. Toast the bread while the fish cooks.

- 8 slices precooked hickory-smoked bacon (such as Jimmy Dean)
- 2 (6-ounce) salmon fillets (about 1 inch thick)
- ¼ teaspoon freshly ground black pepper, divided
- Cooking spray
- ¼ cup light mayonnaise
- 1½ tablespoons fresh lemon juice
- 1½ teaspoons minced fresh dill
- 4 (1-ounce) slices diagonally cut French bread, toasted
- 4 green leaf lettuce leaves
- 4 slices tomato, cut in half

1. Preheat broiler.

2. Microwave bacon slices according to package directions; set aside.

3. While bacon cooks, sprinkle fish with ⅛ teaspoon pepper. Place fish, skin sides down, on a broiler pan coated with cooking spray. Broil 10 to 13 minutes or until fish flakes easily when tested with a fork. Remove skin from fish, and cut fish into chunks.

4. While fish cooks, combine mayonnaise, lemon juice, dill, and remaining ⅛ teaspoon pepper. Spread 1 tablespoon dill mayonnaise on each French bread slice; top with 1 lettuce leaf, 2 tomato halves, 2 slices bacon, and one-fourth of salmon chunks. Drizzle remaining dill mayonnaise over each sandwich. Yield: 4 servings (serving size: 1 sandwich).

Per serving: CALORIES 331 (43% from fat); FAT 15.6g (saturated fat 3g); PROTEIN 24.9g; CARBOHYDRATES 21.4g; FIBER 1.3g; CHOLESTEROL 55mg; IRON 1.7mg; SODIUM 505mg; CALCIUM 31mg

Tomato and Cucumber Salad

prep: 5 minutes   *POINTS* value: 2

In a medium bowl, combine 1 cup halved cherry tomatoes, 2 sliced small salad cucumbers, ½ cup coarsely chopped yellow or green bell pepper, ½ cup light red wine vinaigrette, and ½ teaspoon freshly ground black pepper. Toss well. Cover and chill until ready to serve. Yield: 4 servings (serving size: ¾ cup).

Per serving: CALORIES 66 (71% from fat); FAT 5.2g (saturated fat 0.5g); PROTEIN 0.8g; CARBOHYDRATES 5.6g; FIBER 1.1g; CHOLESTEROL 0mg; IRON 0.3mg; SODIUM 283mg; CALCIUM 12mg

Cornmeal-Crusted Tilapia Sandwiches

prep: 7 minutes • **cook:** 4 minutes   *POINTS* value: 5

A well-seasoned cast-iron skillet will give the fish a crisp crust that resembles the fried version but with less fat. Substitute any firm white fish, such as red snapper or flounder, for the tilapia.

- 3   tablespoons light mayonnaise
- 1   teaspoon minced chipotle chile, canned in adobo sauce
- 3   cups packaged cabbage-and-carrot mix
- 3   tablespoons yellow cornmeal
- ¼   teaspoon freshly ground black pepper
- ½   pound tilapia fillets, cut in half lengthwise
- ⅛   teaspoon salt
- 1   tablespoon canola oil
- 4   (1.5-ounce) white wheat hot dog buns

1. Combine mayonnaise and chile in a large bowl; add cabbage-and-carrot mix, and toss to coat. Set aside.

2. Combine cornmeal and black pepper in a shallow dish. Sprinkle fish with ⅛ teaspoon salt; dredge in cornmeal mixture.

3. Heat oil in a 10-inch cast-iron skillet over medium-high heat. Add fish; cook 2 to 3 minutes on each side or until fish flakes easily when tested with a fork.

4. Divide fish evenly among hot dog buns. Top evenly with cabbage-and-carrot mixture. Serve immediately. Yield: 4 servings (serving size: 1 sandwich).

Per serving: CALORIES 241 (36% from fat); FAT 9.7g (saturated fat 1.1g); PROTEIN 17.3g; CARBOHYDRATES 27.1g; FIBER 5.1g; CHOLESTEROL 32mg; IRON 3.4mg; SODIUM 401mg; CALCIUM 271mg

Menu

POINTS value: 6

Cornmeal-Crusted Tilapia Sandwiches

   1 large peach ☑.
   POINTS value: 1

Grocery List

1 (16-ounce) package cabbage-and-carrot mix

4 large peaches

1 (12-ounce) package white wheat hot dog buns

1 (7.5-ounce) can chipotle chiles in adobo sauce

1 (2-pound) package yellow cornmeal

½ pound tilapia fillets

Check staples: light mayonnaise, canola oil, salt, and black pepper

Grocery List

2 medium lemons

1 small bunch fresh tarragon

1 small bunch fresh flat-leaf parsley

1 (4-ounce) package arugula

1 (10-ounce) package angel hair coleslaw

1 small cucumber

1 small bunch radishes

1 large Fuji apple

1 (24-ounce) package double-fiber bread (such as Arnold)

1 (12-ounce) can chunk white albacore tuna in water

Check staples: light mayonnaise, olive oil, Dijon mustard, and black pepper

Tuna-Tarragon Salad Sandwiches

prep: 9 minutes   *POINTS* value: 6

For a portable meal, place the tuna salad, veggies, bread, and slaw in separate containers and pack them in an insulated bag. Once you're ready to eat, you'll only need to assemble your sandwich.

    1   medium lemon
    ¼   cup light mayonnaise
    1   tablespoon chopped fresh tarragon
    1   teaspoon Dijon mustard
    ⅛   teaspoon freshly ground black pepper
    1   (12-ounce) can chunk white albacore tuna in water, drained
    8   (1½-ounce) slices double-fiber bread (such as Arnold)
    1   cup arugula
    ⅓   cup cucumber slices
    ⅓   cup radish slices

1. Grate 1 teaspoon lemon rind from lemon, and place in a large bowl. Squeeze lemon to extract juice; add 2 teaspoons lemon juice to rind. Add mayonnaise and next 3 ingredients to lemon juice mixture. Gently fold in tuna, breaking into bite-sized pieces.
2. Spread tuna mixture evenly among 4 bread slices; top evenly with arugula, cucumber, and radish. Top with remaining 4 bread slices. Yield: 4 servings (serving size: 1 sandwich).

Per serving: CALORIES 308 (24% from fat); FAT 9.3g (saturated fat 0.8g); PROTEIN 24.8g; CARBOHYDRATES 40.5g; FIBER 10.4g; CHOLESTEROL 31mg; IRON 3.1mg; SODIUM 501mg; CALCIUM 216mg

Tangy Apple Slaw ✔.

prep: 6 minutes   *POINTS* value: 1

Combine 3 cups angel hair coleslaw, 1 seeded and coarsely chopped large Fuji apple, and 2 tablespoons chopped fresh flat-leaf parsley; toss gently. Whisk together 3 tablespoons fresh lemon juice and 1 tablespoon olive oil. Add dressing to slaw mixture, tossing well to coat. Yield: 4 servings (serving size: about 1 cup).

Per serving: CALORIES 74 (41% from fat); FAT 3.6g (saturated fat 0.5g); PROTEIN 0.7g; CARBOHYDRATES 10.9g; FIBER 2.4g; CHOLESTEROL 0mg; IRON 0.2mg; SODIUM 12mg; CALCIUM 7mg

Crab Melts

prep: 3 minutes • **cook:** 4 minutes   *POINTS* value: 5

Sourdough bread is slathered with a cheesy, creamy crab mixture and broiled quickly in the oven until golden. You'll need to use only 2 cups of the crabmeat, so plan to use the rest in the Crab-Stuffed Flounder on page 68.

¼ cup light mayonnaise
2 tablespoons chopped green onions
1½ tablespoons chopped fresh dill
2 teaspoons plain low-fat yogurt
½ teaspoon lemon juice
2 cups lump crabmeat, shell pieces removed (about 12 ounces)
4 (1.3-ounce) slices sourdough bread
4 tablespoons grated fresh Parmesan cheese

1. Preheat broiler.
2. Combine mayonnaise and next 4 ingredients in a medium bowl. Add crabmeat; stir well. Spread crab mixture evenly over bread slices. Sprinkle evenly with Parmesan cheese.
3. Place bread slices on an ungreased baking sheet. Broil 4 to 5 minutes or until cheese is lightly browned. Serve immediately. Yield: 4 servings (serving size: 1 sandwich).

Per serving: CALORIES 247 (28% from fat); FAT 7.5g (saturated fat 1.2g); PROTEIN 23.7g; CARBOHYDRATES 20.7g; FIBER 1.2g; CHOLESTEROL 72mg; IRON 2mg; SODIUM 694mg; CALCIUM 124mg

Watermelon and Watercress Salad

prep: 6 minutes   *POINTS* value: 3

Combine 2 tablespoons olive oil, 2 tablespoons balsamic vinegar, ¼ teaspoon salt, and ⅛ teaspoon freshly ground black pepper in a large bowl; stir well with a whisk. Add 4 cups seeded and cubed watermelon, 2 cups packed watercress, and ½ cup thinly sliced red onion; toss gently to coat. Yield: 4 servings (serving size: 1½ cups).

Per serving: CALORIES 119 (55% from fat); FAT 7.3g (saturated fat 1g); PROTEIN 1.6g; CARBOHYDRATES 14.3g; FIBER 1.1g; CHOLESTEROL 0mg; IRON 0.5mg; SODIUM 156mg; CALCIUM 37mg

Menu

POINTS value: 8

Crab Melts

**Watermelon
and Watercress Salad**

Grocery List

1 small bunch fresh dill

1 small bunch green onions

1 small lemon

1 (32-ounce) container seeded and cubed watermelon

1 (4-ounce) package watercress

1 small red onion

1 (24-ounce) loaf sourdough bread

1 (6-ounce) carton plain low-fat yogurt

1 (8-ounce) wedge Parmesan cheese

1 (16-ounce) container lump crabmeat

Check staples: light mayonnaise, olive oil, balsamic vinegar, salt, and black pepper

Menu

POINTS value: 6

Shrimp Rolls

Pear-Kiwi Salad

Grocery List

1 small lemon

1 large lime

1 small celery stalk

1 small head Boston lettuce

1 small bunch green onions

1 small bunch fresh mint

2 medium pears

4 medium kiwi

1 (12-ounce) package white wheat hot dog buns

¾ pound cooked peeled shrimp

Check staples: light mayonnaise and honey

Shrimp Rolls

prep: 10 minutes   **POINTS** value: 4

We've chosen the traditional hot dog bun or roll for this sandwich. For variety, place a lettuce leaf on top of an 8-inch flour tortilla. Spoon the shrimp mixture onto the lettuce. Roll up the tortilla, secure with a round wooden pick, and cut in half. The POINTS value will be 5.

  1 small lemon

 ¼ cup light mayonnaise

  2 tablespoons chopped green onion tops

 ¾ pound chopped cooked shrimp

 ½ cup finely chopped celery

  4 (1.5-ounce) white wheat hot dog buns

  4 Boston lettuce leaves

1. Grate ½ teaspoon lemon rind from lemon. Squeeze lemon to measure 1½ tablespoons juice. Combine lemon rind, juice, mayonnaise, and green onions in a large bowl. Add shrimp and celery; toss gently.

2. Top each hot dog bun with 1 lettuce leaf. Spoon shrimp mixture evenly onto lettuce leaves. Serve immediately. Yield: 4 servings (serving size: 1 sandwich).

Per serving: CALORIES 220 (30% from fat); FAT 7.4g (saturated fat 1g); PROTEIN 23.1g; CARBOHYDRATES 20.7g; FIBER 4.5g; CHOLESTEROL 171mg; IRON 5.5mg; SODIUM 514mg; CALCIUM 296mg

Pear-Kiwi Salad

prep: 6 minutes   **POINTS** value: 2

Whisk together 2 tablespoons lime juice, 1 tablespoon finely chopped fresh mint, and 1 tablespoon honey in a medium bowl. Add 2 cups sliced pear (about 2 pears) and 1¾ cups sliced peeled kiwi; toss gently. Yield: 4 servings (serving size: ¾ cup).

Per serving: CALORIES 113 (4% from fat); FAT 0.5g (saturated fat 0g); PROTEIN 1.3g; CARBOHYDRATES 29.2g; FIBER 5g; CHOLESTEROL 0mg; IRON 0.4mg; SODIUM 4mg; CALCIUM 36mg

Apple and Cheddar Grilled Cheese

prep: 6 minutes • **cook:** 4 minutes   *POINTS* value: 7

Give a classic grilled cheese sandwich a modern flair by combining sweet, crisp Gala apple slices with Cheddar cheese. A Braeburn or Fuji apple would also work well in this recipe.

2 tablespoons stone-ground Dijon mustard
2 tablespoons light mayonnaise
8 (1-ounce) slices multigrain Italian bread
1 cup (4 ounces) reduced-fat shredded Cheddar cheese, divided
1 medium Gala apple, cored and sliced
Cooking spray

1. Combine mustard and mayonnaise in a small bowl. Spread evenly onto bread slices. Top 4 bread slices with 2 tablespoons cheese, apple slices, 2 tablespoons cheese, and remaining bread slices. Coat both sides of sandwiches with cooking spray.
2. Heat a large nonstick skillet over medium heat. Coat pan with cooking spray. Cook sandwiches 2 to 3 minutes on each side or until golden brown and cheese melts. Yield: 4 servings (serving size: 1 sandwich).

Per serving: CALORIES 311 (32% from fat); FAT 11g (saturated fat 4.9g); PROTEIN 12.8g; CARBOHYDRATES 36.7g; FIBER 3.1g; CHOLESTEROL 23mg; IRON 2mg; SODIUM 784mg; CALCIUM 255mg

Zucchini Chips

prep: 8 minutes • **cook:** 10 minutes   *POINTS* value: 1

Preheat oven to 475°. Coat a baking sheet with cooking spray. Place ½ cup Italian-seasoned breadcrumbs in a shallow dish. Cut 1 large zucchini into ¼-inch slices. Sprinkle ⅛ teaspoon salt and ⅛ teaspoon freshly ground black pepper evenly on zucchini slices. Lightly beat 3 large egg whites. Dip zucchini slices into egg whites, and dredge in breadcrumbs, pressing firmly to coat. Place zucchini slices on prepared baking sheet. Bake at 475° for 10 minutes or until browned, turning once halfway during cooking. Serve immediately. Yield: 4 servings (serving size: about 7 chips).

Per serving: CALORIES 67 (11% from fat); FAT 0.8g (saturated fat 0g); PROTEIN 5.2g; CARBOHYDRATES 10.4g; FIBER 1.3g; CHOLESTEROL 0mg; IRON 0.9mg; SODIUM 284mg; CALCIUM 29mg

Menu

POINTS value: 8

Apple and Cheddar Grilled Cheese

Zucchini Chips

Grocery list

1 medium Gala apple

1 large zucchini

1 (16-ounce) loaf multigrain Italian bread

1 (15-ounce) container Italian-seasoned breadcrumbs

1 (8-ounce) package reduced-fat shredded Cheddar cheese

Check staples: eggs, light mayonnaise, cooking spray, stone-ground Dijon mustard, salt, and black pepper

Menu

POINTS value: 8

Blue Cheese and Pear Sandwiches

White Balsamic–Dill Pasta Salad

Grocery List

1 (4-ounce) package watercress

2 medium pears

1 (8-ounce) container tricolor bell pepper mix

1 small bunch fresh dill

1 (16-ounce) loaf peasant bread

1 (8.5-ounce) bottle white balsamic vinegar

1 (16-ounce) package farfalle (bow tie pasta)

1 (4-ounce) package crumbled blue cheese

Check staples: olive oil, cooking spray, salt, and black pepper

Blue Cheese and Pear Sandwiches

prep: 4 minutes • **cook:** 6 minutes   *POINTS* value: 4

This recipe is a salad and sandwich in one: a hearty slice of peasant bread topped with sweet pears, pungent blue cheese, and peppery watercress. Look for artisan peasant bread in the bakery at your supermarket.

> 4   (1½-ounce) slices peasant bread
> Cooking spray
> 1⅓ cups coarsely chopped watercress
> 2   teaspoons olive oil
> ⅛   teaspoon salt
> ⅛   teaspoon freshly ground black pepper
> 2   medium pears, thinly sliced
> ½   cup (2 ounces) crumbled blue cheese

1. Preheat broiler.

2. Place bread slices on a baking sheet. Coat each slice with cooking spray; broil 2 minutes on each side or until lightly toasted.

3. While bread cooks, combine watercress, olive oil, salt, and pepper in a small bowl; toss gently.

4. Place pear slices evenly on bread slices; top with blue cheese. Broil 2 to 3 minutes or until cheese melts. Remove from oven; top with watercress mixture. Serve immediately. Yield: 4 servings (serving size: 1 sandwich).

Per serving: CALORIES 211 (29% from fat); FAT 6.9g (saturated fat 3g); PROTEIN 7.5g; CARBOHYDRATES 31.7g; FIBER 2.5g; CHOLESTEROL 11mg; IRON 1.2mg; SODIUM 506mg; CALCIUM 139mg

White Balsamic–Dill Pasta Salad

prep: 2 minutes • **cook:** 14 minutes   *POINTS* value: 4

Cook 2 cups uncooked farfalle (bow tie pasta) according to package directions, omitting salt and fat. Rinse under cold water until cool; drain well. While pasta cooks, whisk together 2 tablespoons white balsamic vinegar, 1 tablespoon olive oil, ⅛ teaspoon salt, and ⅛ teaspoon freshly ground black pepper in a medium bowl. Add pasta, ½ cup pre-chopped tricolor bell pepper mix, and 1 tablespoon chopped fresh dill; toss well. Yield: 4 servings (serving size: ¾ cup).

Per serving: CALORIES 196 (19% from fat); FAT 4.1g (saturated fat 0.7g); PROTEIN 6g; CARBOHYDRATES 34g; FIBER 1.7g; CHOLESTEROL 0mg; IRON 1.5mg; SODIUM 77mg; CALCIUM 12mg

Greek-Style Hummus Wraps

prep: 10 minutes   *POINTS* value: 6

Greek-style hummus provides a delicious and satisfying base for this veggie sandwich. Look for it in the deli section of your supermarket.

  1 (7-ounce) container Greek-style hummus (such as Athenos)
  4 (7-inch) low-fat flour tortillas
1⅓ cups diced tomato
1⅓ cups shredded lettuce
1⅓ cups sliced cucumber
  ½ cup (2 ounces) crumbled feta cheese

1. Spread hummus evenly over tortillas. Top evenly with tomato and remaining ingredients. Roll up; secure ends with wooden picks. Yield: 4 servings (serving size: 1 wrap).

Per serving: CALORIES 291 (35% from fat); FAT 11.2g (saturated fat 2.8g); PROTEIN 11.3g; CARBOHYDRATES 39.8g; FIBER 6.1g; CHOLESTEROL 17mg; IRON 2.8mg; SODIUM 839mg; CALCIUM 204mg

Minted Melon and Fennel Salad ☑.

prep: 5 minutes   *POINTS* value: 1

Combine 1 cup chopped cantaloupe, 1 cup mixed baby greens, ½ cup thinly sliced fennel bulb, and 2 tablespoons chopped fresh mint in a medium bowl. Combine 1 tablespoon white wine vinegar, 2 teaspoons olive oil, and ¼ teaspoon freshly ground black pepper in a small bowl, stirring with a whisk. Pour vinegar mixture over cantaloupe mixture, tossing to coat. Yield: 4 servings (serving size: ½ cup).

Per serving: CALORIES 40 (56% from fat); FAT 2.5g (saturated fat 0.4g); PROTEIN 0.7g; CARBOHYDRATES 4.6g; FIBER 0.7g; CHOLESTEROL 0mg; IRON 0.4mg; SODIUM 16mg; CALCIUM 18mg

Menu

POINTS value: 7

Greek-Style Hummus Wraps

Minted Melon and Fennel Salad

Grocery List

1 medium tomato

1 (8-ounce) package shredded lettuce

1 (4-ounce) package mixed baby greens

1 small cucumber

1 (16-ounce) container chopped cantaloupe

1 small fennel bulb

1 small bunch fresh mint

1 (17.5-ounce) package (7-inch) low-fat flour tortillas

1 (7-ounce) container Greek-style hummus (such as Athenos)

1 (4-ounce) package crumbled feta cheese

Check staples: olive oil, white wine vinegar, and black pepper

Menu

POINTS value: 7

Grilled Portobello Burritos

Cilantro-Lime Mango

Grocery List

4 large portobello caps

1 (24-ounce) jar refrigerated mango

1 small red onion

3 medium limes

1 small bunch fresh cilantro

1 (7-ounce) container hummus

1 (4-ounce) package pine nuts

1 (12.7-ounce) package (8½-inch) spinach tortillas

1 (4-ounce) package crumbled feta cheese

Check staples: olive oil–flavored cooking spray, salt, and black pepper

Grilled Portobello Burritos

prep: 8 minutes • **cook:** 10 minutes   *POINTS* value: 6

The portobello mushroom's steaklike texture and earthy flavor make it a natural choice for this vegetarian sandwich. Spinach tortillas add extra flavor and color to the burritos, but you may substitute low-fat flour tortillas.

  4 large portobello caps
     Olive oil–flavored cooking spray
  ¼ teaspoon salt
  ¼ teaspoon freshly ground black pepper
  ½ cup hummus
  4 (8½-inch) spinach tortillas, warmed
  ¼ cup (1 ounce) crumbled feta cheese
  ¼ cup pine nuts, toasted

1. Prepare grill.

2. Coat both sides of mushrooms with cooking spray; sprinkle with salt and pepper.

3. Grill mushrooms 5 minutes on each side or until tender. Cut mushrooms into ¼-inch strips. Spread hummus evenly over warm tortillas; divide mushrooms evenly among center of tortillas. Sprinkle evenly with cheese and pine nuts. Fold top and bottom of each tortilla toward center. Roll up; secure ends with wooden picks. Yield: 4 servings (serving size: 1 burrito).

Per serving: CALORIES 281 (42% from fat); FAT 13.1g (saturated fat 2.3g); PROTEIN 10.6g; CARBOHYDRATES 33.9g; FIBER 3.6g; CHOLESTEROL 8mg; IRON 4.1mg; SODIUM 521mg; CALCIUM 155mg

Cilantro-Lime Mango

prep: 3 minutes   *POINTS* value: 1

Combine 2 cups refrigerated jarred mango, ¼ cup thinly sliced red onion, ¼ cup fresh lime juice, and 2 tablespoons chopped fresh cilantro in a medium bowl; toss gently to coat. Yield: 4 servings (serving size: ½ cup).

Per serving: CALORIES 77 (0% from fat); FAT 0g (saturated fat 0g); PROTEIN 0.2g; CARBOHYDRATES 21g; FIBER 0.7g; CHOLESTEROL 0mg; IRON 0mg; SODIUM 16mg; CALCIUM 4mg

Roast Beef Sandwiches

prep: 5 minutes • **cook:** 20 seconds   *POINTS* value: 5

Our warm and saucy roast beef sandwich is a healthy alternative to its fast food cousin because it contains 50% less fat and sodium. This sandwich is delicious topped with both the barbecue sauce and the horseradish sauce or served with just one.

½ pound low-sodium thinly sliced deli roast beef (such as Boar's Head)
4 (1.8-ounce) white wheat hamburger buns
¼ cup light mayonnaise
1 tablespoon prepared horseradish
¼ teaspoon freshly ground black pepper
¼ cup barbecue sauce (such as Stubb's)

1. Microwave roast beef and buns at HIGH for 20 seconds or until warm.
2. Combine mayonnaise, horseradish, and pepper in a small bowl, stirring with a spoon. Top each bun evenly with roast beef, horseradish sauce, and barbecue sauce. Yield: 4 servings (serving size: 1 sandwich).

Per serving: CALORIES 241 (36% from fat); FAT 9.7g (saturated fat 2.5g); PROTEIN 20.8g; CARBOHYDRATES 2.5g; FIBER 5.2g; CHOLESTEROL 36mg; IRON 4.2mg; SODIUM 548mg; CALCIUM 253mg

Cucumber and Onion Salad

prep: 6 minutes   *POINTS* value: 0

Whisk together ½ cup white wine vinegar and 2 teaspoons sugar in a medium bowl. Add 1 medium English cucumber, halved lengthwise and sliced; 1 vertically sliced small red onion; and 1 tablespoon chopped fresh parsley. Toss to coat. Serve immediately, or cover and chill until ready to serve. Yield: 4 servings (serving size: ¾ cup).

Per serving: CALORIES 22 (4% from fat); FAT 0.1g (saturated fat 0g); PROTEIN 10.6g; CARBOHYDRATES 5.2g; FIBER 0.7g; CHOLESTEROL 0mg; IRON 0.2mg; SODIUM 2mg; CALCIUM 13mg

Menu

POINTS value: 5

Roast Beef Sandwiches

Cucumber and Onion Salad

Grocery List

1 medium English cucumber

1 small red onion

1 small bunch fresh parsley

1 (12-ounce) package white wheat hamburger buns

½ pound low-sodium thinly sliced deli roast beef (such as Boar's Head)

1 (5.25-ounce) jar prepared horseradish

1 (18-ounce) bottle barbecue sauce (such as Stubb's)

Check staples: light mayonnaise, white wine vinegar, sugar, and black pepper

Menu

POINTS value: 7

Greek Chicken Salad Pitas

1 cup red grapes ✔.
POINTS value: 1

Grocery List

1 (22-ounce) package hearts of romaine

1 small cucumber

1 small red onion

1 medium lemon

1 pound seedless red grapes

1 (12-ounce) package (6-inch) whole wheat pitas

1 (2-pound) rotisserie chicken

1 (4-ounce) package crumbled feta cheese

1 (7-ounce) container roasted red bell pepper hummus

Check staples: olive oil, salt, and black pepper

Greek Chicken Salad Pitas

prep: 11 minutes   *POINTS* value: 6

You'll find prepared hummus in a variety of flavors. We used a roasted red bell pepper hummus for this sandwich, but a spicy three-pepper or an artichoke-and-garlic hummus would be a good choice, too.

  2 cups sliced romaine lettuce
  1 cup chopped roasted chicken breast
  ⅔ cup diced seeded cucumber
  ¼ cup thinly sliced red onion
  ¼ cup (1 ounce) crumbled feta cheese
  2 tablespoons fresh lemon juice
  2 tablespoons olive oil
  ¼ teaspoon salt
  ¼ teaspoon freshly ground black pepper
  6 tablespoons roasted red bell pepper hummus
  2 (6-inch) whole wheat pitas, cut in half

1. Combine lettuce and next 4 ingredients in a large bowl. Add lemon juice, olive oil, salt, and pepper; toss gently.

2. Spread 1½ tablespoons hummus inside each pita half; spoon salad mixture evenly into halves. Serve immediately. Yield: 4 servings (serving size: 1 pita half).

Per serving: CALORIES 278 (44% from fat); FAT 13.5g (saturated fat 2.9g); PROTEIN 16.7g; CARBOHYDRATES 24.6g; FIBER 4.1g; CHOLESTEROL 38mg; IRON 2mg; SODIUM 669mg; CALCIUM 71mg

Spicy Chicken Wraps

prep: 15 minutes

POINTS value: 6

Wrap these spicy and crunchy sandwiches individually in parchment paper or wax paper to hold them together for easier eating on the go or for packing in a lunch bag or picnic basket.

- ¼ cup light mayonnaise
- 2 tablespoons chili garlic sauce
- 4 multigrain wraps (such as Flatout)
- 2 cups chopped roasted chicken breast
- 1 cup thinly sliced romaine lettuce
- 1 cup matchstick-cut carrots
- 1 cup sliced green onions (about 7)

1. Combine mayonnaise and chili garlic sauce in a small bowl; spread evenly over half of each wrap. Top mayonnaise mixture evenly with chicken and remaining ingredients. Roll up; secure ends with wooden picks. Yield: 4 servings (serving size: 1 wrap).

Per serving: CALORIES 289 (31% from fat); FAT 10.1g (saturated fat 1.5g); PROTEIN 31.8g; CARBOHYDRATES 24.2g; FIBER 9.9g; CHOLESTEROL 65mg; IRON 2.8mg; SODIUM 887mg; CALCIUM 63mg

Pineapple-Basil Salad

prep: 3 minutes

POINTS value: 1

Combine 2 cups cubed fresh pineapple, 2 teaspoons finely chopped fresh basil, 1 teaspoon sugar, and 1 teaspoon fresh lime juice in a medium bowl; toss to coat. Yield: 4 servings (serving size: ½ cup).

Per serving: CALORIES 42 (2% from fat); FAT 0.1g (saturated fat 0g); PROTEIN 0.4g; CARBOHYDRATES 11g; FIBER 1.1g; CHOLESTEROL 0mg; IRON 0.2mg; SODIUM 1mg; CALCIUM 11mg

Menu

POINTS value: 7

Spicy Chicken Wraps

Pineapple-Basil Salad

Grocery List

1 (22-ounce) package hearts of romaine

1 (10-ounce) package matchstick-cut carrots

1 medium bunch green onions

1 (16-ounce) container cubed fresh pineapple

1 small lime

1 small bunch fresh basil

1 (11.4-ounce) package multigrain wraps (such as Flatout)

1 (2-pound) rotisserie chicken

1 (10.7-ounce) bottle chili garlic sauce

Check staples: light mayonnaise and sugar

pictured on page 122

Honey Barbecue Chicken Sandwiches

prep: 4 minutes • **cook:** 1 minute • **other:** 10 minutes   *POINTS* value: 7

A Southern specialty, this sandwich is often made with chicken or pork that has been cooked slowly over low heat. To deliver a juicy barbecue sandwich with a similar flavor but a faster prep time, we used a store-bought rotisserie chicken purchased from the deli.

1   (10-ounce) package angel hair coleslaw
⅓   cup light coleslaw dressing
6   (1.6-ounce) light wheat hamburger buns, toasted
3   cups shredded roasted chicken
6   tablespoons honey barbecue sauce

1. Combine coleslaw and dressing in a bowl, tossing well. Let stand 10 minutes.
2. Top bottom half of each bun with ½ cup chicken, 1 tablespoon barbecue sauce, and ½ cup coleslaw mixture. Place top halves of buns on top of coleslaw mixture. Serve immediately. Yield: 6 servings (serving size: 1 sandwich).

Per serving: CALORIES 345 (24% from fat); FAT 9.2g (saturated fat 1.9g); PROTEIN 25.4g; CARBOHYDRATES 39.1g; FIBER 4.5g; CHOLESTEROL 72mg; IRON 2.1mg; SODIUM 791mg; CALCIUM 59mg

Tomato and Watermelon Salad

prep: 4 minutes   *POINTS* value: 1

Combine 4 cups cubed seeded watermelon, 2 coarsely chopped medium tomatoes, ½ cup thinly sliced red onion, and 2 tablespoons chopped fresh basil in a medium bowl; toss gently. Drizzle ¼ cup light red wine vinaigrette over salad; toss to coat. Serve immediately. Yield: 6 servings (serving size: 1 cup).

Per serving: CALORIES 62 (28% from fat); FAT 1.9g (saturated fat 0.2g); PROTEIN 1.2g; CARBOHYDRATES 11.6g; FIBER 1.3g; CHOLESTEROL 0mg; IRON 0.4mg; SODIUM 97mg; CALCIUM 17mg

Menu

POINTS value: 8

Honey Barbecue Chicken Sandwiches

Tomato and Watermelon Salad

Grocery List

1 (10-ounce) package angel hair coleslaw

1 (32-ounce) container cubed seeded watermelon

2 medium tomatoes

1 small red onion

1 small bunch fresh basil

1 (12-ounce) package light wheat hamburger buns

1 (2-pound) rotisserie chicken

1 (16-ounce) bottle light coleslaw dressing

1 (16-ounce) bottle light red wine vinaigrette

1 (18-ounce) bottle honey barbecue sauce

Tarragon Chicken Burgers

prep: 3 minutes • **cook:** 14 minutes
POINTS value: 5

When buying ground chicken, make sure that the label reads "ground chicken breast" rather than "ground chicken." The fat and calorie savings are significant.

1¼ pounds ground chicken breast
¼ cup finely chopped green onions
 1 teaspoon dried tarragon
½ teaspoon salt
¼ teaspoon freshly ground black pepper
  Cooking spray
¼ cup light mayonnaise
 4 (1.5-ounce) light wheat hamburger buns, toasted
  Curly leaf lettuce, tomato slices, and red onion slices (optional)

1. Combine first 5 ingredients in a medium bowl. Divide into 4 equal portions; shape each into a 1-inch-thick patty.

2. Heat a large nonstick skillet over medium heat. Coat pan with cooking spray. Add burgers, and cook 7 to 8 minutes on each side or until done.

3. Spread mayonnaise evenly on both halves of each bun. Place 1 burger patty on bottom half of each bun; top each patty with lettuce, tomato, and red onion, if desired. Place top halves of buns on burgers. Yield: 4 servings (serving size: 1 burger).

Per serving: CALORIES 251 (23% from fat); FAT 6.7g (saturated fat 1g); PROTEIN 34.5g; CARBOHYDRATES 21.8g; FIBER 4.3g; CHOLESTEROL 87mg; IRON 1.7mg; SODIUM 678mg; CALCIUM 51mg

Broccoli-Cranberry Salad

prep: 5 minutes • **cook:** 2 minutes
POINTS value: 3

Combine ⅓ cup light mayonnaise and 1 tablespoon sugar in a medium bowl. Coarsely chop 4 cups broccoli florets. Combine broccoli with ⅓ cup dried cranberries; ¼ cup sliced green onions; and 2 teaspoons toasted, salted sunflower seed kernels. Toss well to coat. Yield: 4 servings (serving size: 1 cup).

Per serving: CALORIES 141 (49% from fat); FAT 7.7g (saturated fat 1.1g); PROTEIN 2.6g; CARBOHYDRATES 17.7g; FIBER 3.1g; CHOLESTEROL 7mg; IRON 0.9mg; SODIUM 181mg; CALCIUM 43mg

Menu

POINTS value: 8

Tarragon Chicken Burgers

Broccoli-Cranberry Salad

Grocery List

1 small bunch green onions

1 small head curly leaf lettuce (optional)

1 medium tomato (optional)

1 small red onion (optional)

1 (12-ounce) package broccoli florets

1 (12-ounce) package light wheat hamburger buns

1 (7.25-ounce) package salted sunflower seed kernels

1 (6-ounce) package dried cranberries

1¼ pounds ground chicken breast

Check staples: light mayonnaise, cooking spray, sugar, dried tarragon, salt, and black pepper

pictured on page 41

Grilled Chicken and Tomato Pesto Baguettes

prep: 7 minutes • **cook:** 8 minutes

Menu

Grilled Chicken and Tomato Pesto Baguettes

1 cup mixed raw orange bell peppers slices, baby green beans, and zucchini slices ☑.

POINTS value: 0

Grocery List

1 medium red bell pepper

1 medium orange bell pepper

1 small head curly leaf lettuce

1 (8-ounce) package baby green beans

1 small zucchini

1 (8.5-ounce) thin whole wheat baguette

1 (10-ounce) jar sun-dried tomato pesto (such as Classico)

1 (8-ounce) package sliced low-fat Swiss cheese

2 (8-ounce) skinless, boneless chicken breast halves

Check staples: cooking spray, salt, and black pepper

Work quickly when assembling the sandwich so that the grilled chicken and bell pepper retain enough heat from grilling to melt the cheese.

  1 (8.5-ounce) thin whole wheat baguette
  2 (8-ounce) skinless, boneless chicken breast halves
¼ teaspoon salt
⅛ teaspoon black pepper
  1 red bell pepper, seeded and quartered
Cooking spray
¼ cup sun-dried tomato pesto (such as Classico)
  4 curly leaf lettuce leaves
  4 (0.7-ounce) slices low-fat Swiss cheese, cut in half lengthwise

1. Prepare grill.

2. Cut baguette in half lengthwise. Hollow out top half of baguette, leaving a ½-inch border; reserve torn bread for another use. Set aside.

3. Place chicken breast halves between 2 large sheets of heavy-duty plastic wrap; pound to ½-inch thickness using a meat mallet or small heavy skillet. Sprinkle chicken with salt and pepper.

4. Flatten bell pepper quarters with hands. Coat chicken breasts and bell pepper quarters with cooking spray; place on grill rack. Cover and grill 8 minutes or until chicken is done and bell peppers are tender, turning once. Place cut sides of baguette halves on grill during last 2 minutes of grilling to lightly toast. Cut each chicken breast in half crosswise.

5. Spread both cut halves of baguette evenly with pesto. Top bottom half with lettuce leaves, chicken halves, bell pepper quarters, and cheese slices. Place top half of baguette on top of cheese. Cut crosswise into 4 equal portions. Yield: 4 servings (serving size: ¼ of baguette).

Per serving: CALORIES 345 (19% from fat); FAT 7.2g (saturated fat 3.2g); PROTEIN 39.3g; CARBOHYDRATES 24.7g; FIBER 1.7g; CHOLESTEROL 66mg; IRON 2.4mg; SODIUM 748mg; CALCIUM 271mg

Soups

Grilled Salmon Chowder

1 cup baby spinach and
spring mix salad with
fat-free balsamic vinaigrette ☑.

POINTS value: 0

Grocery List

1 small bunch green onions

1 (5.5-ounce) package baby
spinach and spring mix

1 (14-ounce) can fat-free,
less-sodium chicken broth

1 (8-ounce) bottle fat-free
balsamic viniagrette

1 (10-ounce) box oyster crackers
(optional)

1 (24-ounce) container refrigerated mashed potatoes (such as
Simply Potatoes)

1 (6.3-ounce) package frozen
grilled salmon (such as Gorton's)

1 (24-ounce) package frozen
shoepeg corn

Check staples: 2% reduced-fat
milk, salt, and black pepper

Grilled Salmon Chowder

prep: 2 minutes • **cook:** 11 minutes   *POINTS* value: 4

The frozen grilled salmon offers convenience and brings a surprisingly rich flavor to this chowder. If you prefer a thicker consistency, simply stir ½ cup of oyster crackers into each serving for an additional *POINTS* value of 2.

1½   cups refrigerated mashed potatoes (such as Simply Potatoes)
1½   cups 2% reduced-fat milk
  1   cup fat-free, less-sodium chicken broth
  1   (6.3-ounce) package frozen grilled salmon (such as Gorton's)
1½   cups frozen shoepeg corn, thawed
  ½   teaspoon freshly ground black pepper
  ¼   teaspoon salt
  2   tablespoons chopped green onions
  Oyster crackers (optional)

1. Bring potatoes, milk, and broth to a boil over medium-high heat in a large saucepan; cover, reduce heat, and simmer 5 minutes or until slightly thick.
2. While potato mixture cooks, heat fish in microwave according to package directions; flake into bite-sized pieces.
3. Add corn, pepper, and salt to potato mixture; bring to a boil, stirring frequently. Add fish; simmer 1 minute or until fish is heated. Stir in green onions, and ladle soup into bowls. Serve with oyster crackers, if desired. Yield: 4 servings (serving size: 1¼ cups).

Per serving: CALORIES 207 (20% from fat); FAT 4.6g (saturated fat 1.4g); PROTEIN 14.5g; CARBOHYDRATES 26.6g; FIBER 2.7g; CHOLESTEROL 24mg; IRON 0.5mg; SODIUM 677mg; CALCIUM 125mg

Coconut Shrimp Soup

prep: 3 minutes • **cook:** 6 minutes   *POINTS* value: 5

Light coconut milk adds subtle coconut flavor to this spicy soup for two. Use a vegetable peeler to remove the strip of rind from the lime, but be careful to avoid the white pith because it can be very bitter.

- 1   cup light coconut milk
- 1   cup water
- ½   teaspoon red curry paste
- ¼   teaspoon salt
- 1   (2 x ½–inch) strip lime rind
- ¾   pound peeled and deveined large shrimp
- ¼   cup julienne-cut fresh basil

1. Combine first 5 ingredients in a large saucepan, stirring with a whisk. Bring to a boil over medium-high heat. Add shrimp; cover, reduce heat to medium, and cook 3 minutes or until shrimp turn pink. Remove and discard lime rind; stir in basil. Yield: 2 servings (serving size: 1⅔ cups).

Per serving: CALORIES 199 (34% from fat); FAT 7.5g (saturated fat 6.1g); PROTEIN 28.7g; CARBOHYDRATES 5.2g; FIBER 0.4g; CHOLESTEROL 252mg; IRON 4.7mg; SODIUM 633mg; CALCIUM 61mg

Edamame Salad

prep: 5 minutes   *POINTS* value: 3

Place 1 cup frozen shelled edamame and ¾ cup frozen petite corn kernels in a colander, and rinse under cool running water to thaw; drain well. Combine edamame, corn, ¼ cup chopped red onion, 1 tablespoon chopped fresh parsley or cilantro, and 1½ tablespoons light olive oil vinaigrette in a medium bowl; toss well to coat. Serve immediately, or cover and chill until ready to serve. Yield: 2 servings (serving size: 1 cup).

Per serving: CALORIES 152 (31% from fat); FAT 5.6g (saturated fat 0.2g); PROTEIN 8g; CARBOHYDRATES 19.9g; FIBER 3.8g; CHOLESTEROL 0mg; IRON 1.4mg; SODIUM 95mg; CALCIUM 43mg

---

Menu

POINTS value: 8

Coconut Shrimp Soup

Edamame Salad

Grocery List

1 small lime

1 small bunch fresh basil

1 small bunch fresh parsley or cilantro

1 small red onion

1 (13.5-ounce) can light coconut milk

1 (4-ounce) jar red curry paste

1 (16-ounce) bottle light olive oil vinaigrette

1 (12-ounce) package frozen shelled edamame

1 (12-ounce) package frozen petite corn kernels

¾ pound peeled and deveined large shrimp

Check staples: salt

Menu

POINTS value: 4

Black Bean Soup with Salsa

Toasted Lime Tortilla Crisps

Grocery List

1 small onion

1 whole garlic head

1 (16-ounce) container refrigerated fresh salsa

1 (8.5-ounce) package (7-inch) flour tortillas (such as Azteca)

1 (14-ounce) can fat-free, less-sodium chicken broth

2 (14.5-ounce) cans black beans

1 (0.49-ounce) package crystallized lime (such as True Lime)

1 (8-ounce) carton reduced-fat sour cream

1 (8-ounce) package reduced-fat shredded Cheddar cheese

Check staples: cooking spray and salt

Black Bean Soup with Salsa

prep: 3 minutes • **cook:** 12 minutes   *POINTS* value: 3

We blended 2 cups of the bean mixture to give extra body to this soup. You can vary the heat with your choice of salsa. Be sure to use a refrigerated fresh salsa because it has 50% less sodium than bottled salsa.

Cooking spray
1 cup diced onion
4 garlic cloves, minced
2 (14.5-ounce) cans black beans, rinsed and drained
1 (14-ounce) can fat-free, less-sodium chicken broth
½ cup refrigerated fresh salsa
¼ cup reduced-fat sour cream
¼ cup (1 ounce) reduced-fat shredded Cheddar cheese

1. Heat a large saucepan over medium-high heat. Coat pan with cooking spray. Add onion, and cook 5 minutes; add garlic, and cook 1 minute. Add beans and broth to pan. Cover and bring to a boil; reduce heat, and simmer 5 minutes.
2. Place 2 cups soup in a blender. Remove center piece of blender lid (to allow steam to escape); secure blender lid on blender. Place a clean towel over opening in blender lid (to avoid splatters). Blend until smooth. Return pureed soup to pan; stir well. Ladle into bowls, and top with salsa, sour cream, and cheese. Yield: 4 servings (serving size: 1 cup soup, 2 tablespoons salsa, 1 tablespoon sour cream, and 1 tablespoon cheese).

Per serving: CALORIES 155 (20% from fat); FAT 3.4g (saturated fat 2.2g); PROTEIN 9.7g; CARBOHYDRATES 25.2g; FIBER 7.1g; CHOLESTEROL 11mg; IRON 2.1mg; SODIUM 760mg; CALCIUM 123mg

Toasted Lime Tortilla Crisps

prep: 4 minutes • **cook:** 4 minutes   *POINTS* value: 1

Preheat oven to 425°. Stack 4 (7-inch) flour tortillas (such as Azteca) on a work surface. Cut stack into 6 wedges. Arrange wedges on a parchment paper–lined baking sheet. Coat wedges with cooking spray. Combine 2 packets crystallized lime (such as True Lime) and ¼ teaspoon salt in a small bowl; sprinkle over wedges. Bake at 425° for 3 minutes or just until chips become golden. Turn chips, and bake 1 minute. Remove from oven, and let stand on baking sheet until crisp. Yield: 4 servings (serving size: 6 chips).

Per serving: CALORIES 77 (20% from fat); FAT 1.7g (saturated fat 0.3g); PROTEIN 2g; CARBOHYDRATES 13.5g; FIBER 1g; CHOLESTEROL 0mg; IRON 0.8mg; SODIUM 305mg; CALCIUM 0mg

Curried Chickpea and Vegetable Stew ☑

prep: 4 minutes • **cook:** 3 hours, 40 minutes   *POINTS* value: 4

The individual flavors of these few ingredients have a chance to blend and mellow as they simmer in the slow cooker, creating a simple, tasty vegetarian stew. For a complete meal, serve over cooked couscous.

    2 (16-ounce) cans chickpeas (garbanzo beans), rinsed and drained
    1 (14.5-ounce) can diced tomatoes, undrained
    ½ (16-ounce) package frozen bell pepper and onion stir-fry
    ¼ cup water
    4 teaspoons curry powder
    ½ teaspoon salt
    ⅛ teaspoon black pepper
    1 (5- or 6-ounce) package fresh baby spinach

1. Combine first 7 ingredients in a 4-quart electric slow cooker; stir well. Cover and cook on HIGH 3½ hours. Add spinach; cover and cook 10 minutes or until spinach wilts. Serve immediately. Yield: 4 servings (serving size: 1¼ cups).

Per serving: CALORIES 218 (15% from fat); FAT 3.7g (saturated fat 0g); PROTEIN 9.6g; CARBOHYDRATES 38.2g; FIBER 10.8g; CHOLESTEROL 0mg; IRON 4.7mg; SODIUM 690mg; CALCIUM 121mg

Menu

POINTS value: 6

Curried Chickpea and Vegetable Stew

½ cup couscous
POINTS value: 2

Grocery List

1 (5- or 6-ounce) package fresh baby spinach

2 (16-ounce) cans chickpeas (garbanzo beans)

1 (14.5-ounce) can diced tomatoes

1 (10-ounce) box uncooked plain couscous

1 (16-ounce) package frozen bell pepper and onion stir-fry

Check staples: curry powder, salt, and black pepper

Grocery List

1 medium red onion

1 (5- or 6-ounce) package fresh baby spinach

1 whole garlic head

1 (16-ounce) loaf ciabatta

1 (16-ounce) package dried lentils

1 (14.5-ounce) can no-salt-added diced tomatoes

Check staples: olive oil, olive oil–flavored cooking spray, balsamic vinegar, salt, and black pepper

Warm Lentil Stew ☑.

prep: 2 minutes • **cook:** 38 minutes   *POINTS* value: 2

Lentils, members of the legume family (which includes beans, peas, and soybeans), are a great source of protein and fiber. They add a mild, nutty flavor to this soup. Unlike some other legumes, lentils cook quickly and don't require soaking. Add the spinach leaves toward the end of cooking to keep their color bright.

Olive oil–flavored cooking spray
- 1   medium red onion, chopped (about 2 cups)
- 4   cups water
- ½   cup dried lentils
- 1   (14.5-ounce) can no-salt-added diced tomatoes, undrained
- ¾   teaspoon salt
- 1   (5- or 6-ounce) package fresh baby spinach
- 1½   tablespoons balsamic vinegar
- ½   teaspoon freshly ground black pepper

1. Heat a Dutch oven over medium heat. Coat pan with cooking spray. Add onion, and sauté 4 minutes.

2. Add water and next 3 ingredients. Cover and bring to a boil; boil 30 minutes or until lentils are tender. Stir in spinach, vinegar, and pepper; cook 1 minute or until spinach wilts. Serve immediately. Yield: 4 servings (serving size: 1¼ cups).

Per serving: CALORIES 163 (5% from fat); FAT 0.1g (saturated fat 0g); PROTEIN 9.9g; CARBOHYDRATES 33.8g; FIBER 8.3g; CHOLESTEROL 0mg; IRON 4mg; SODIUM 549mg; CALCIUM 66mg

Garlic Ciabatta Toast

prep: 5 minutes • **cook:** 4 minutes   *POINTS* value: 3

Prepare broiler. Cut 4 (¾-inch-thick) slices from a ciabatta loaf. Brush 1 tablespoon olive oil evenly over both sides of ciabatta slices. Crush 1 garlic clove using a garlic press, and spread garlic evenly over 1 side of each bread slice. Broil 2 minutes on each side or until toasted. Sprinkle garlic sides evenly with ⅛ teaspoon pepper and ¹⁄₁₆ teaspoon salt. Yield: 4 servings (serving size: 1 slice).

Per serving: CALORIES 128 (35% from fat); FAT 5g (saturated fat 0.7g); PROTEIN 3.1g; CARBOHYDRATES 19g; FIBER 0.6g; CHOLESTEROL 0mg; IRON 1.1mg; SODIUM 269mg; CALCIUM 3mg

Split Pea Soup ☑

prep: 10 minutes • **cook:** 8 hours   *POINTS* value: 4

Come home to a steaming bowl of satisfying split pea soup. Instead of using the standard stove-top method, you can let the slow cooker cook the soup while you are at work. This soup is great the day after you make it; thin it with water as you reheat it.

- 6 cups fat-free, less-sodium chicken broth
- 1 (16-ounce) package green split peas
- 2 carrots, peeled and chopped
- 2 celery stalks, chopped (about ⅔ cup)
- 1 small onion, finely chopped
- ¾ teaspoon salt
- ¼ teaspoon black pepper

1. Combine all ingredients in a 3- to 4-quart electric slow cooker. Cover and cook on LOW 8 hours. Yield: 8 servings (serving size: 1 cup).

Per serving: CALORIES 216 (3% from fat); FAT 0.7g (saturated fat 0.1g); PROTEIN 16.5g; CARBOHYDRATES 37.6g; FIBER 15.2g; CHOLESTEROL 0mg; IRON 2.6mg; SODIUM 673mg; CALCIUM 43mg

Garlic-Parmesan Cheese Toast

prep: 2 minutes • **cook:** 6 minutes   *POINTS* value: 3

Preheat oven to 400°. Combine ½ cup (2 ounces) shredded fresh Parmesan cheese, 2 tablespoons light mayonnaise, 2 minced garlic cloves, and ¼ teaspoon freshly ground black pepper in a small bowl. Spread cheese mixture evenly onto 8 (¾-inch-thick) slices diagonally cut French bread baguette. Place bread on a baking sheet coated with cooking spray. Bake at 400° for 6 minutes or until bread is golden brown and cheese melts. Yield: 8 servings (serving size: 1 slice).

Per serving: CALORIES 130 (27% from fat); FAT 3.9g (saturated fat 1.4g); PROTEIN 5.7g; CARBOHYDRATES 18.5g; FIBER 0.7g; CHOLESTEROL 8mg; IRON 1mg; SODIUM 327mg; CALCIUM 131mg

Menu
POINTS value: 7

Split Pea Soup

Garlic-Parmesan Cheese Toast

Grocery List

1 (16-ounce) bag carrots

1 small bunch celery

1 small onion

1 whole garlic head

1 (12-ounce) French bread baguette

2 (32-ounce) cartons fat-free, less-sodium chicken broth

1 (16-ounce) package green split peas

1 (8-ounce) wedge Parmesan cheese

Check staples: light mayonnaise, cooking spray, salt, and black pepper

Grocery List

1 small onion

1 whole garlic head

1 large jalapeño pepper

1 (14.5-ounce) can diced
tomatoes

1 (8-ounce) package semisweet
chocolate

1 (16-ounce) package self-rising
white cornmeal mix

1 (1-quart) carton fat-free
buttermilk

1 pound ground round

Check staples: eggs, canola
oil, cooking spray, chili powder,
ground cumin, dried oregano,
and salt

Mexican Chili

prep: 3 minutes • **cook:** 15 minutes   *POINTS* value: 3

Chocolate is often added to savory dishes in Mexican cuisine to cut the heat and enrich the flavor. In this recipe, it adds richness and deepens the color of the chili without being sweet.

- 1   pound ground round
- 1   cup chopped onion (about 1 small onion)
- 1   garlic clove, minced
- 1   (14.5-ounce) can diced tomatoes, undrained
- 1   cup water
- 2   tablespoons chili powder
- 1   ounce semisweet chocolate, coarsely chopped
- 1   teaspoon ground cumin
- 1   teaspoon salt
- ½   teaspoon dried oregano

1. Cook beef in a large saucepan over medium-high heat until browned, stirring to crumble. Drain, if necessary, and return beef to pan. Add onion and garlic to pan; cook 4 minutes or until tender. Add tomatoes and remaining ingredients; cover and simmer 7 minutes. Serve immediately. Yield: 6 servings (serving size: ¾ cup).

Per serving: CALORIES 136 (31% from fat); FAT 4.7g (saturated fat 2.1g); PROTEIN 17.3g; CARBOHYDRATES 8.2g; FIBER 1.8g; CHOLESTEROL 40mg; IRON 1.9mg; SODIUM 597mg; CALCIUM 25mg

Jalapeño Corn Bread Mini Muffins

prep: 9 minutes • **cook:** 17 minutes   *POINTS* value: 3

Preheat oven to 425°. Lightly spoon ¾ cup self-rising white cornmeal mix into measuring cups; level with a knife, and place in a large bowl. Combine ½ cup fat-free buttermilk, 2 tablespoons minced seeded jalapeño pepper, 1½ tablespoons canola oil, and 1 large egg in a small bowl. Pour buttermilk mixture into cornmeal mixture; stir just until combined. Spoon batter evenly into 12 miniature muffin cups coated with cooking spray. Bake at 425° for 17 minutes or until lightly browned. Remove from pans immediately; serve warm. Yield: 6 servings (serving size: 2 mini muffins).

Per serving: CALORIES 127 (34% from fat); FAT 4.8g (saturated fat 0.5g); PROTEIN 3.7g; CARBOHYDRATES 17.4g; FIBER 1.3g; CHOLESTEROL 30mg; IRON 1.2mg; SODIUM 312mg; CALCIUM 93mg

pictured on page 117

Beef and Vegetable Soup

prep: 5 minutes • **cook:** 25 minutes   *POINTS* value: 4

Warm up to our speedy version of this classic homestyle favorite. Frozen vegetables shave minutes off the prep time, while the jarred pasta sauce adds a depth of flavor. Serve the soup with crispy whole wheat saltine crackers.

  1   pound ground sirloin
  ½   cup chopped red onion (about 1 small onion)
  2   (14-ounce) cans fat-free, less-sodium beef broth
  1   cup water
  1   (26-ounce) jar pasta sauce with bell peppers, onions, and spices
       (such as Newman's Own Sockarooni)
  1   (16-ounce) package frozen mixed vegetables
  ¼   teaspoon black pepper

1. Cook beef and onion in a large Dutch oven over medium-high heat until browned, stirring to crumble beef. Drain, if necessary, and return beef mixture to pan. Stir in broth and remaining ingredients; cover and bring to a boil. Uncover, reduce heat, and simmer 15 minutes or until thoroughly heated. Yield: 8 servings (serving size: about 1 cup).

Per serving: CALORIES 191 (30% from fat); FAT 6.3g (saturated fat 2g); PROTEIN 14.8g; CARBOHYDRATES 17.8g; FIBER 2.3g; CHOLESTEROL 35mg; IRON 2.5mg; SODIUM 613mg; CALCIUM 21mg

Menu

POINTS value: 5

Beef and Vegetable Soup

5 whole wheat saltine crackers
POINTS value: 1

Grocery List

1 small red onion

2 (14-ounce) cans fat-free, less-sodium beef broth

1 (26-ounce) jar pasta sauce with bell peppers, onions, and spices (such as Newman's Own Sockarooni)

1 (16-ounce) box whole wheat saltine crackers

1 (16-ounce) package frozen mixed vegetables

1 pound ground sirloin

Check staples: black pepper

POINTS value: 7

Quick Posole

Fiesta Tortilla Chips

Grocery List

1 small bunch fresh cilantro (optional)

1 (8.5-ounce) package (7-inch) flour tortillas (such as Azteca)

1 (14.5-ounce) can zesty chili-style diced tomatoes (such as Del Monte)

1 (14-ounce) can fat-free, less-sodium beef broth

1 (15.5-ounce) can white hominy

1 (8-ounce) carton reduced-fat sour cream (optional)

1 pound lean ground pork

Check staples: cooking spray, salt-free Mexican seasoning, and salt

Quick Posole

prep: 2 minutes • **cook:** 13 minutes   *POINTS* value: 6

A traditional posole's signature ingredients are pork, hominy, and dried chiles. Mexican cooks often spend up to 2 days preparing the hominy by pounding and soaking the corn kernels. Here, we've used a can of hominy and chili-style diced tomatoes to simplify the preparation.

  1 pound lean ground pork
  1 tablespoon salt-free Mexican seasoning
  1 (15.5-ounce) can white hominy, rinsed and drained
  1 (14.5-ounce) can zesty chili-style diced tomatoes (such as Del Monte), undrained
  1 (14-ounce) can fat-free, less-sodium beef broth
Reduced-fat sour cream (optional)
Chopped fresh cilantro (optional)

1. Cook pork in a large saucepan over medium-high heat until browned, stirring to crumble. Drain, if necessary, and return pork to pan. Sprinkle pork with Mexican seasoning, and cook, stirring constantly, over medium-high heat 30 seconds.

2. Stir in hominy, tomatoes, and broth. Cover and bring to a boil; reduce heat, and simmer 5 minutes. Ladle into bowls, and top with sour cream and cilantro, if desired. Yield: 4 servings (serving size: 1½ cups).

Per serving: CALORIES 266 (38% from fat); FAT 11.3g (saturated fat 4.3g); PROTEIN 26g; CARBOHYDRATES 15.4g; FIBER 3.1g; CHOLESTEROL 85mg; IRON 0.9mg; SODIUM 686mg; CALCIUM 26mg

Fiesta Tortilla Chips

prep: 4 minutes • **cook:** 4 minutes   *POINTS* value: 1

Preheat oven to 425°. Stack 4 (7-inch) flour tortillas (such as Azteca) on a work surface. Cut stack into 6 wedges. Arrange wedges on a parchment paper–lined baking sheet. Coat wedges with cooking spray. Sprinkle with 1½ teaspoons salt-free Mexican seasoning and ⅛ teaspoon salt. Coat again lightly with cooking spray. Bake at 425° for 3 minutes or just until chips become golden. Turn chips, and bake 1 minute. Remove from oven, and let stand on baking sheet until crisp. Yield: 4 servings (serving size: 6 chips).

Per serving: CALORIES 77 (20% from fat); FAT 1.7g (saturated fat 0.3g); PROTEIN 2g; CARBOHYDRATES 13.5g; FIBER 1g; CHOLESTEROL 0mg; IRON 0.8mg; SODIUM 233mg; CALCIUM 0mg

Greens, Beans, and Bacon Soup

prep: 3 minutes • **cook:** 36 minutes   *POINTS* value: 4

This hearty soup is chock-full of antioxidants and fiber from the kale and beans, and it pairs well with a crunchy slice of toasted ciabatta. Look for a package of prechopped kale in the produce section of your supermarket.

  3 slices lower-sodium bacon, cut crosswise into ¼-inch pieces
  3 cups packed prechopped kale
2¼ cups water
  1 (15-ounce) can no-salt-added cannellini beans, rinsed and drained
  1 (14.5-ounce) can roasted garlic chicken broth
  1 cup frozen chopped onion
  ¼ teaspoon black pepper
      Hot sauce (optional)

1. Cook bacon in a large saucepan over medium-high heat 8 minutes or until crisp. Reserve 2 teaspoons drippings in pan; discard excess drippings.
2. Add kale and next 5 ingredients to bacon and drippings in pan. Stir in hot sauce, if desired. Cover and bring to a boil over high heat. Reduce heat, and simmer 25 minutes. Serve immediately. Yield: 3 servings (serving size: 1⅔ cups).

Per serving: CALORIES 200 (36% from fat); FAT 8.1g (saturated fat 2.3g); PROTEIN 10.5g; CARBOHYDRATES 23.2g; FIBER 5.5g; CHOLESTEROL 15mg; IRON 2.9mg; SODIUM 792mg; CALCIUM 127mg

Menu

POINTS value: 6

Greens, Beans, and Bacon Soup

1 (1-ounce) slice toasted ciabatta
***POINTS* value: 2**

Grocery List

1 (16-ounce) package prechopped kale

1 (16-ounce) loaf ciabatta

1 (14.5-ounce) can roasted garlic chicken broth

1 (15-ounce) can no-salt-added cannellini beans

1 (2-ounce) bottle hot sauce (optional)

1 (10-ounce) package frozen chopped onion

1 (16-ounce) package lower-sodium bacon

Check staples: black pepper

Menu

POINTS value: 6

Sweet Pea Soup with Bacon

1 (1.25-ounce) slice toasted
multigrain bread
POINTS value: 2

Grocery List

1 (24-ounce) loaf multigrain
bread

1 (32-ounce) carton fat-free,
less-sodium chicken broth

1 (20-ounce) package refrigerated diced potatoes with onions
(such as Simply Potatoes)

1 (16-ounce) carton fat-free
half-and-half

1 (16-ounce) package frozen
petite green peas

1 (16-ounce) package lower-
sodium bacon

Check staples: black pepper

Sweet Pea Soup with Bacon

prep: 5 minutes • **cook:** 35 minutes   *POINTS* value: 4

Half-and-half and refrigerated potatoes add creamy, rich texture to this soup, while the bacon adds crunch and smoky flavor.

6	slices lower-sodium bacon
1½	cups refrigerated diced potatoes with onions (such as Simply Potatoes)
4	cups fat-free, less-sodium chicken broth
1	(16-ounce) package frozen petite green peas
½	cup fat-free half-and-half
¼	teaspoon freshly ground black pepper

1. Cook bacon in a large Dutch oven over medium-high heat 8 minutes or until crisp. Drain bacon on a paper towel; crumble. Reserve 2 tablespoons drippings in pan; discard excess drippings.

2. Add potatoes to drippings in pan, and sauté 5 minutes or until slightly brown. Add broth and peas to pan; bring to a boil. Cover, reduce heat to medium-low, and simmer 15 minutes. Place 4½ cups soup in a blender. Remove center piece of blender lid (to allow steam to escape); secure blender lid on blender. Place a clean towel over opening in blender lid (to avoid splatters). Blend until smooth. Return pureed soup to pan; add half-and-half and pepper. Heat 4 minutes or until thoroughly heated. Ladle soup into bowls, and top evenly with crumbled bacon. Yield: 6 servings (serving size: 1 cup soup and 1 tablespoon bacon).

Per serving: CALORIES 194 (38% from fat); FAT 7.9g (saturated fat 2.8g); PROTEIN 9.7g; CARBOHYDRATES 20g; FIBER 4g; CHOLESTEROL 13mg; IRON 1.4mg; SODIUM 637mg; CALCIUM 31mg

pictured on page 39

Ham and Butternut Squash Soup

prep: 2 minutes • **cook:** 8 minutes   *POINTS* value: 4

Celebrate fall all year long with the help of frozen butternut squash. This sweet-savory soup has a velvety appearance and texture.

2 (12-ounce) packages frozen butternut squash (such as McKenzie's)
1 cup fat-free, less-sodium chicken broth
2 tablespoons cinnamon sugar
½ teaspoon black pepper
2 teaspoons olive oil
1½ cups diced ham (such as Cumberland Gap)
1 tablespoon chopped fresh rosemary

1. Microwave packages of squash at HIGH 5 minutes or until thawed. Combine squash with broth, cinnamon sugar, and pepper in a large microwave-safe bowl. Microwave at HIGH 3 to 5 minutes or until thoroughly heated.

2. While squash mixture cooks, heat oil in a large nonstick skillet over medium-high heat. Pat ham dry with paper towels. Add ham to pan, and cook 2 minutes or until lightly browned. Add rosemary, and cook 1 minute, stirring occasionally.

3. Ladle soup into bowls, and sprinkle ham topping evenly in center of each bowl. Yield: 4 servings (serving size: about ¾ cup soup and 3 tablespoons ham topping).

Per serving: CALORIES 185 (37% from fat); FAT 7.6g (saturated fat 1.2g); PROTEIN 9.9g; CARBOHYDRATES 19.8g; FIBER 2.6g; CHOLESTEROL 19mg; IRON 2.2mg; SODIUM 828mg; CALCIUM 55mg

Menu

POINTS value: 5

Ham and Butternut Squash Soup

2 multigrain crispbreads
POINTS value: 1

Grocery List

1 small bunch fresh rosemary

1 (14-ounce) can fat-free, less-sodium chicken broth

1 (3.6-ounce) jar cinnamon sugar

1 (8.8-ounce) package multi-grain crispbreads (such as Wasa)

2 (12-ounce) packages frozen butternut squash (such as McKenzie's)

1 (8-ounce) package diced ham (such as Cumberland Gap)

Check staples: olive oil and black pepper

Menu

POINTS value: 5

Asian Chicken, Edamame, and Noodle Soup

2 small plums ☑.
POINTS value: 1

Grocery List

12 small plums

1 (10-ounce) package refrigerated cooked shelled edamame

1 small bunch green onions

1 (2-pound) rotisserie chicken

1 (32-ounce) carton fat-free, less-sodium chicken broth

1 (3-ounce) package teriyaki chicken–flavored ramen noodles

Asian Chicken, Edamame, and Noodle Soup

prep: 3 minutes • **cook:** 20 minutes   *POINTS* value: 4

Edamame (green soybeans) are often served in Japanese restaurants and are quickly becoming readily available in most supermarkets. Look for refrigerated cooked shelled edamame in the produce section at your supermarket. Substitute the frozen uncooked variety for the refrigerated version, if desired.

- 2 cups chopped roasted chicken breast
- 1 (10-ounce) package refrigerated cooked shelled edamame
- 1 (32-ounce) carton fat-free, less-sodium chicken broth
- 1 (3-ounce) package teriyaki chicken–flavored ramen noodles
- 1 cup thinly sliced green onions

1. Combine first 3 ingredients in a Dutch oven; bring to a boil. Cover, reduce heat to low, and simmer 12 minutes. Break noodles into 1-inch pieces. Add noodles, contents of flavoring packet, and green onions to pan; cook 3 minutes. Serve immediately. Yield: 6 servings (serving size: about 1 cup).

Per serving: CALORIES 219 (25% from fat); FAT 5.9g (saturated fat 1.6g); PROTEIN 23.8g; CARBOHYDRATES 16.2g; FIBER 3.3g; CHOLESTEROL 40mg; IRON 2.2mg; SODIUM 888mg; CALCIUM 51mg

Creamy Chicken and Corn Chowder

prep: 5 minutes • **cook:** 15 minutes   *POINTS* value: 6

Knock the chill off a cold winter's night with this simple yet satisfying homemade soup. Convenience items from your grocery store will help you prepare this recipe in minutes.

1 (10-ounce) package frozen vegetable seasoning blend
1 (20-ounce) package frozen cream-style corn (such as McKenzie's), thawed
2 cups chopped roasted chicken breast
1 cup frozen extrasweet whole-kernel corn
2 cups fat-free, less-sodium chicken broth

1. Combine all ingredients in a Dutch oven. Bring to a boil; cover, reduce heat, and simmer 10 minutes, stirring occasionally. Serve immediately. Yield: 4 servings (serving size: 1¾ cups).

Per serving: CALORIES 316 (8% from fat); FAT 2.9g (saturated fat 0.7g); PROTEIN 26.6g; CARBOHYDRATES 42.7g; FIBER 4.3g; CHOLESTEROL 60mg; IRON 1.3mg; SODIUM 839mg; CALCIUM 37mg

Menu

POINTS value: 6

Creamy Chicken and Corn Chowder

1 cup field greens salad with fat-free red wine vinaigrette ✓.

POINTS **value: 0**

Grocery List

1 (8-ounce) bag fresh field greens

1 (2-pound) rotisserie chicken

1 (8-ounce) bottle fat-free red wine vinaigrette

1 (14-ounce) can fat-free, less-sodium chicken broth

1 (10-ounce) package frozen vegetable seasoning blend

1 (20-ounce) package frozen cream-style corn (such as McKenzie's), thawed

1 (10-ounce) package frozen extrasweet whole-kernel corn

Menu

POINTS value: 5

Chicken Florentine Soup

1 (1-ounce) slice whole wheat
baguette
POINTS value: 1

Grocery List

1 (5- or 6-ounce) package fresh
baby spinach

1 (8.5-ounce) thin whole wheat
baguette

1 (32-ounce) carton fat-free,
less-sodium chicken broth

1 (14.5-ounce) can diced
tomatoes with basil, garlic,
and oregano

1 (10-ounce) jar commercial
pesto

1 (16-ounce) package ditalini
(very short tube-shaped
macaroni)

1 (8-ounce) wedge Parmesan
cheese (optional)

1¼ pounds skinless, boneless
chicken thighs

Check staples: black pepper

Chicken Florentine Soup

prep: 5 minutes • **cook:** 13 minutes   *POINTS* value: 4

Warm crusty bread is all you need to round out this rustic one-dish meal. Use it to soak up the richly flavored broth. Orzo makes a fine substitute for the ditalini.

½ cup uncooked ditalini (very short tube-shaped macaroni)
1¼ pounds skinless, boneless chicken thighs, chopped
3 cups fat-free, less-sodium chicken broth
1 cup water
1 (14.5-ounce) can diced tomatoes with basil, garlic, and oregano
1 (5- or 6-ounce) package fresh baby spinach
2 tablespoons commercial pesto
¼ teaspoon freshly ground black pepper
Grated fresh Parmesan cheese (optional)

1. Cook pasta according to package directions, omitting salt and fat. Set aside.
2. While pasta cooks, combine chicken, chicken broth, and water in a Dutch oven. Cover, and bring to a boil. Reduce heat, and simmer 3 minutes or until chicken is cooked. Remove chicken with a slotted spoon; keep warm. Stir in tomatoes; cook 1 minute or until thoroughly heated. Stir in spinach; cook 2 minutes or until spinach wilts. Add cooked chicken and pasta to pan; cook 1 minute or until thoroughly heated. Stir in pesto and pepper. Ladle soup into bowls, and sprinkle with Parmesan cheese, if desired. Yield: 6 servings (serving size: 1½ cups).

Per serving: CALORIES 219 (25% from fat); FAT 6.2g (saturated fat 1.4g); PROTEIN 23.7g; CARBOHYDRATES 17.1g; FIBER 2.4g; CHOLESTEROL 80mg; IRON 3.3mg; SODIUM 810mg; CALCIUM 88mg

Index

10 Simple Core Plan® Side Dishes

Vegetable	Servings	Preparation	Cooking Instructions
Asparagus	3 to 4 per pound	Snap off tough ends. Remove scales, if desired.	To steam: Cook, covered, on a rack above boiling water 2 to 3 minutes. To boil: Cook, covered, in a small amount of boiling water 2 to 3 minutes or until crisp-tender.
Broccoli	3 to 4 per pound	Remove outer leaves and tough ends of lower stalks. Wash; cut into spears.	To steam: Cook, covered, on a rack above boiling water 5 to 7 minutes or until crisp-tender.
Carrots	4 per pound	Scrape; remove ends, and rinse. Leave tiny carrots whole; slice large carrots.	To steam: Cook, covered, on a rack above boiling water 8 to 10 minutes or until crisp-tender. To boil: Cook, covered, in a small amount of boiling water 8 to 10 minutes or until crisp-tender.
Cauliflower	4 per medium head	Remove outer leaves and stalk. Wash. Break into florets.	To steam: Cook, covered, on a rack above boiling water 5 to 7 minutes or until crisp-tender.
Corn	4 per 4 large ears	Remove husks and silks. Leave corn on the cob, or cut off kernels.	Cook, covered, in boiling water to cover 8 to 10 minutes (on cob) or in a small amount of boiling water 4 to 6 minutes (kernels).
Green beans	4 per pound	Wash; trim ends, and remove strings. Cut into 1½-inch pieces.	To steam: Cook, covered, on a rack above boiling water 5 to 7 minutes. To boil: Cook, covered, in a small amount of boiling water 5 to 7 minutes or until crisp-tender.
Potatoes	3 to 4 per pound	Scrub; peel, if desired. Leave whole, slice, or cut into chunks.	To boil: Cook, covered, in boiling water to cover 30 to 40 minutes (whole) or 15 to 20 minutes (slices or chunks). To bake: Bake at 400° for 1 hour or until done.
Snow peas	4 per pound	Wash; trim ends, and remove tough strings.	To steam: Cook, covered, on a rack above boiling water 2 to 3 minutes. Or sauté in cooking spray or 1 teaspoon oil over medium-high heat 3 to 4 minutes or until crisp-tender.
Squash, summer	3 to 4 per pound	Wash; trim ends, and slice or chop.	To steam: Cook, covered, on a rack above boiling water 6 to 8 minutes. To boil: Cook, covered, in a small amount of boiling water 6 to 8 minutes or until crisp-tender.
Squash, winter *(including acorn, butternut, and buttercup)*	2 per pound	Rinse; cut in half, and remove all seeds. Leave in halves to bake, or peel and cube to boil.	To boil: Cook cubes, covered, in boiling water 20 to 25 minutes. To bake: Place halves, cut sides down, in a shallow baking dish; add ½ inch water. Bake, uncovered, at 375° for 30 minutes. Turn and season, or fill; bake an additional 20 to 30 minutes or until tender.